ESL Games : 176 English Language Games for Children

SHELLEY ANN VERNON

2nd Edition 2012
3rd Edition 2015
4th Edition September 2015

ISBN: 1475255586
ISBN-13: 978-1475255584

Available in Spanish - ISBNs: 1514391767 / 978-1514391761
Available in Italian - ISBNs: 1515262790 / 978-1515262794

CONTENTS

ACKNOWLEDGMENTS

Since the first edition of this book many teachers have written to me with stories of their successes, adaptations and game ideas. With each new edition improvements have been made based on those practical tips and recommendations. Many thanks therefore to all the teachers who wrote to me with ideas, stories and classroom fun, which can now be shared with you.

THE PHILOSOPHY BEHIND THE GAMES

Please note that this book is written with British spelling.

Thank you for having bought this book of games. It is good to know that you will soon be bringing more success and joy into the lives of children you teach. Consequently you'll be more satisfied as a teacher.

It's true for many that we never forget our teachers. We even remember the ordinary ones, who were unimaginative or just went through the motions, and we feel grateful for the few teachers who challenged us and made us think, rather than spoon fed us so we could regurgitate our answers over the exam paper to get a reasonable grade and then forget everything immediately afterwards!

Many children have great difficulty learning English in school, despite taking lessons several times a week for years. Languages are often taught in school in the same way as other subjects, following a textbook and focusing on reading and writing. While written exams might be two hours long the oral evaluation is a few minutes. As a result of this, teaching time is usually divided up in the same way with 90% of the class time spent reading textbooks and doing writing assignments.

This does not reflect our pupils' needs. What child learns his or her mother tongue by first sitting with a textbook reading out paragraphs? Absolutely no one, obviously. Children already understand and speak their native language before learning to read and write it. Yet typically there is little speaking time in a language class. Consequently this book contains more listening and speaking games than reading and writing activities because the skill of speaking is the most neglected in classes today.

These games are a tool to multiply the talking time of your class exponentially. Pupils will pass their written exams and also be able to speak English. This is because the games are designed to have as many people talking at once in a controlled environment in terms of the language used and in terms of keeping discipline in class.

There are no arts and crafts activities in this book. When time is short children will learn more English from a game drill than they will from making things.

Don't think that games are time-fillers or treats for good behaviour. These games are far more effective than passive teaching methods so use several in every lesson. The games are tried and tested and work for many reasons. Here are some of them to inspire you to take the plunge and use a new game in your next class:

Fun: Games make learning fun. When children enjoy the class they identify with the subject, pay more attention and do better.

Purpose: Playing a game has a purpose to it, an outcome. Pupils will need to say things in order to play the game rather than repeat them back mindlessly, or with no real reason to communicate.

Movement: The physical movement involved in some of the games helps keep everyone alert and focused. Children naturally have a lot of energy and are not good at sitting for long periods so when you throw in a game with movement from time to time it prevents them from getting restless and bored.

Repetition: Another reason these games work is that they involve frequent repetition, which is the mother of skill. We remember things by making a special mental effort to retain them and also by frequent exposure. Repetition can be boring but in the context of these games it is disguised or given a purpose. Repetition is an integral part of most of the games, thereby guaranteeing maximum exposure to whatever language you are teaching.

Revision: In addition the games lend themselves perfectly to quick bursts of revision. Revise a whole topic in a five-minute game. Using games to revise two or three topics every lesson, as well as teaching the latest topic will help pupils remember the whole syllabus, not just what was covered in the last lesson. As a consequence they will do much better at exam time.

Create a teacher-student bond: Playing games in class will engage your students and undoubtedly you will create a closer bond with them. They will respect you more and grow to love you. Ultimately this is what gives you satisfaction as a teacher, alongside seeing your students achieve through your guidance.

Games also create a relaxed atmosphere in class where children will feel that it is OK to try rather than fearing failure. You'll also find even the shy students will join in and become motivated. Over all your students will find learning English more accessible and more fun.

Learning styles: Games tap into the different learning styles of your pupils. It is well researched that using more than one style increases the overall rate of learning since the lesson will resonate with more pupils in your class. Be sure to use a great variety of games and not always the same ones. By varying the games from this book you will appeal to the auditory, visual, kinaesthetic and tactile learning styles.

The teacher's attitude is a key to success.

Games are fun but this doesn't mean the teacher has to be a clown. Smile and be yourself. Be firm and business-like. Using games does not mean English class is recreation.

Always encourage the children, and make them feel that they are doing well. A child who gets poor grades all the time or who is always way down the list in class will tend to stay there as their self-esteem drops lower and lower. A friend of mine told me the story of how he always 0 out of 20 in Latin so he asked his father, a professor of Latin and Ancient Greek, to do his homework for him. Result: 0.5 out of 20. His father went in to see the school Latin teacher and found himself obliged to give her a lesson in Latin. From this point on the friend got 6 out of 20, as the teacher did not dare go any lower. So don't be like that Latin teacher! If most of your pupils are doing poorly then either your assignments are not suitable or your preparation is inadequate, but either way, you are partially responsible for your students' grades!

While you can't do the work for your students, since it is in their hands whether or not they apply themselves and make the mental effort required of them, you can certainly motivate and make it easier for them so they have every chance to succeed. I'll never forget a parent coming to me at the end of two terms and telling me how her daughter, who had learning difficulties, had gained so much in confidence since coming to my classes that she had improved across the board in all subjects at school. I had of course noticed that the child in question did indeed have a problem since she could not remember anything for more than a few seconds, while the children around her were retaining the words and phrases. I never let on that I had noticed, and would frequently ask her questions where the answer had only just been used by one of the other children. I heaped praise on her when she got it right, and she felt good coming to my classes. She felt like she was doing well and gained confidence in herself, which had a knock-on effect in all her academic development.

The games in this book, when used successfully, will improve your pupils' confidence, motivation, behaviour and retention of language. If you have not used games before in class you will be surprised to see how motivated the children become, because they have a reason to pay attention that they relate to – a game! If they do not pay attention during the presentation of new language and make a mental effort, they will not be able to play the games well, and they'll let their team and themselves down. You will find that the use of games during class stimulates and motivates your children to new levels, even the shy ones will participate and naughty pupils will settle down.

These games are going to be another string to your bow to allow you to feel the joy of teaching, and the satisfaction of being successful in your mission. Your pupils will love you. Your head of school, if you have one, will appreciate you immensely as a valuable member of the team. But most of all you are going to know that you have made a great contribution to the world by spreading love through your encouragement and lively, inspiring teaching, and you'll treasure the thanks and appreciation that will come your way.

QUICK START GUIDE AND DETAILED INDEX

1. Step One: Listening games to introduce new language
2. Step Two: Listening games to consolidate
3. Step Three: Easy speaking games
4. Step Four: More demanding speaking games
5. Step Five: Reading
6. Step Six: Spelling and writing games
7. Games ideal for specific language or grammar
8. Games ideal for playing with songs or rhymes
9. Games to use with older children or adults

It is vital that you play enough listening games for pupils to recognise the words before proceeding to speaking games. Keep it simple and build progressively so that everyone has fun. If a game is not working it is most likely because the children cannot handle the language well enough yet. If you rush to a speaking or writing game before the children have taken the new language or vocabulary on board the game will fail.

It is highly recommended to use steps one to three in order, to give the children the best chance of remembering what they learn and being able to use it in the subsequent steps. Steps 4 to 6 may be used in any order.

Step 1: Listening games to introduce new vocabulary and language

Before playing any games you need to present the vocabulary for the first time. Do this by holding up a picture, pointing to the item and naming it. Have the class repeat the word back to you in unison. Do this twice per word for three words. Then start an easy listening game right away. As you play the game feed in more new words. Hold up the new picture card, name the word and feed it right into the game. Each time you introduce new words vary the listening game so it does not become a dull routine.

With 4 year olds, introduce three words to start with, and play some games just with those three words. With older children introduce 6 new words, play games with those and add more if you see your class can easily handle it. A good tactic is to use 6 new words and 6 words that are revision. When introducing new grammar use known vocabulary so not every element is new.

The best games to use during the presentation stage of new vocabulary are:

Commands Race
    Class: any Space: aisles Pace: flexible Level: easy
Copycat Commands
    Class: any Space: noPace: wake up Level: easy
Decoding
    Class: any Space: noPace: calm Level: easy
Draw
    Class: any Space: noPace: wake up Level: easy
Head to Head
    Class: 4 to 30 Space: flexible Pace: excitable Level: easy
Jump the line
    Class: any Space: flexible Pace: wake up Level: easy
Match & Mirroring
    Class: any Space: no Pace: wake up Level: flexible
Musical Vocabulary
    Class: 2 to 30 Space: yes Pace: wake up Level: easy
Pronunciation Hands Up

Class: 2 to 40 Space: no Pace: calm Level: easy
Pronunciation Word Stress
Class: any Space: no Pace: wake up Level: easy
Rapid Grab It
Class: 2 to 20 Space: no Pace: wake up Level: easy
Rapid Reaction
Class: 2 to 16 Space: circle game Pace: wake up Level: easy
Recognising Tenses
Class: any Space: flexible Pace: wake up Level: easy
Show Me
Class: any Space: flexible Pace: wake up Level: easy
Team Race Listening
Class: 1 to 30 Space: yes Pace: excitable Level: easy
The Big Freeze
Class: any Space: flexible Pace: calm Level: easy
Upside Down Game
Class: 2 to 15 Space: no Pace: wake up Level: easy

Step 2: More listening games to consolidate new language

Once you have introduced the maximum number of words your group can handle play more listening games that require a slightly better grip of the words.

These games also allow for fun and effective revision of many words in a short space of time. It is useful to refresh your pupils' memories with a quick listening game before any speaking activity.

Abracadanagram A
Class: 2 to 30 Space: No Pace: wake up Level: flexible
Abracadanagram B
Class: any Space: no Pace: calm Level: flexible
All Change
Class: 6 to 20 Space: yes Pace: excitable Level: flexible
Bingo
Class: any Space: no Pace: calm Level: easy
Board Bash

Class: 2 to 30 Space: no Pace: calm Level: easy

Colour Wolf

Class: any Space: flexible Pace: flexible Level: easy

Flashcard Chase

Class: 3 to 20 Space: yes Pace: Lively Level: easy

Ladders Basic

Class: 8 to 40 Space: yes Pace: excitable Level: easy

Phoneme Wall Chart

Class: 1 to 35 Space: aisles Pace: wake up Level: easy

Simon Says

Class: any Space: no Pace: wake up Level: easy

Team race Q & A

Class: 2 to 30 Space yes Pace: excitable Level: easy

Team Race on Board

Class: 2 to 30 Space: no Pace: wake up Level: easy

True or False

Class: any Space: No Pace: Calm Level: easy

Vocabulary Revision Snap

Class: any Space: No Pace: wake up Level: easy

Where Is It?

Class: 2 to 30 Space: no Pace: calm Level: flexible

Step 3: Games for communicating with new language

Once your class or group have become proficient at listening and understanding the new vocabulary or language structure you are presenting, proceed to some speaking games.

Abracadanagram B

Class: any Space: no Pace: calm - wake up Level: flexible

Abracadanagram C

Class: any Space: no Pace: flexible Level: flexible

Action Race

Class: 2 to 40 Space: aisles Pace: wake up Level: easy

All Change speaking

Class: 6 to 20 Space: yes Pace: excitable Level: easy

Alphabet B

Class: 2 to 30 Space: no Pace: calm Level: flexible

Backwards Bull's Eye

Class: 2 to 30 Space: no Pace: calm Level: flexible

Balloon Fortunes

Class: 4 to 30 Space: aisles Pace: wake up Level: flexible

Blind Painter

Class: 2 to 30 Space no Pace: wake up Level: easy

British Bulldog Basic

Class: 5 to 30 Space: yes Pace: excitable Level: easy

Call My Bluff

Class: Any Space: No Pace: Calm Level: easy

Chanting Game

Class: 2 to 15 Space flexible Pace: wake up Level: easy

Chinese Whispers

Class: any Space: no Pace: calm Level: easy

Dancing Demons

Class: 3 to 21 Space: yes Pace: wake up Level: easy

Duck, Duck Goose

Class: any Space: yes Pace: wake up Level: easy

Find the Pairs

Class: 2 to 40 Space: Some Pace: calm Level: flexible

Find Your Friend

Class: 6 to 40 Space: aisles Pace: wake up Level: flexible

Flashcard Chase

Class: small group or class Space: yes Pace: wake up Level: easy

Gorilla

Class: flexible Space: flexible Pace: wake up or excitable Level: easy

Go to the Vocab

Class: 4 to 20 Space: yes Pace: wake up Level: easy

Grandma's Footsteps

Class: 4 to any Space: no Pace: wake up Level: easy

Guess the Action

Class: 4 to 40 Space: flexible Pace: wake up Level: easy

Hangman

Class: 2 to 30 Space: no Pace: calm Level: easy

Hangman Variant
Class: 2 to 30 Space: no Pace: calm Level: Flexible
Hidden Picture A
Class: 1 to 30 Space: no Pace: wake up Level: easy
Hot Potato
Class: 5 to any Space: no Pace: wake up Level: easy
Jackpot
Class: 3 to 35 Space: no Pace: calm Level: easy
Joker
Class: small group Space: to sit in group Pace: calm Level: easy
Jungle Treasure
Class: 8 to 20 Space: yes Pace: wake up Level: flexible
Kidnap
Class: 12 to any Space: no Pace: wake up Level: easy
Ladders Q & A
Class: 8 to 40 Space: yes Pace: excitable Level: easy
Miming Games
Class: 2 to 40 Space: flexible Pace: wake up Level: flexible
Mystery Bag
Class: 2 to 30 Space: no Pace: calm Level: easy
Noughts & Crosses
Class: pair work Space: no Pace: Calm Level: flexible
One Lemon
Class: 4 to 35 Space: no Pace: Calm Level: easy
Oranges
Class: 6 to 40 Space: aisles Pace: wake up Level: flexible
Spoon Game
Class: 4 to 15 Space: sit in circle Pace: wake up Level: easy
Pass the Box
Class: 4 to 40 Space: flexible Pace: wake up Level: easy
Pass the Parcel
Class: 3 to 30 Space: flexible Pace: calm Level: flexible
Pass the Pictures
Class: 5 to 40 Space: no Pace: wake up Level: easy

Phoneme Hangman
Class: 1 to 30 Space: no Pace: calm Level: phonemes
Phoneme Race
Class: 2 to 40 Space: no Pace: calm Level: phonemes
Phoneme Wall Chart
Class: 1 to 35 Space: aisles Pace: wake up Level: easy
Pictionary
Class: 2 to 40 Space: group work Pace: wake up
Level: easy
Piggy in the Middle
Class: 4 to 15 Space: Yes Pace: wake up Level: easy
Piggy Variant
Class: 4 to 15 Space: yes Pace: wake up Level: easy
Ping Pang Pong
Class: Up to 30 Space: no Pace: calm Level: easy
Preposition Mimes
Class: Any Space: aisles Pace: wake up Level: easy
Pronunciation Chart
Class: 2 to 40 Space: no Pace: calm Level: any
Pronunciation Feather
Class: 2 to 40 Space: no Pace: calm Level: p, b & h
Pronunciation Game
Class: 2 to 40 Space: no Pace: calm Level: any
Pronunciation Picture
Class: 2 to 40 Space: no Pace: calm Level: any
Proverb Pairs
Class: any Space: no Pace: calm Level: medium
Question & Answer
Class: any Space: no Pace: calm Level: easy
Q & A Lottery
Class: any Space: no Pace: calm Level: flexible
Rapid Reaction A
Class: 2 to 16 Space: flexible Pace: wake up Level: easy
Relay Race
Class: any Space: flexible Pace: wake up Level: easy
Scissors Paper Stone
Class: 2 to 40 Space: aisles OK Pace: calm Level: easy

Shopping Memory
Class: 2 to 40 Space no Pace: calm Level: flexible
Snowballs
Class: 2 to 30 Space aisles Pace: wake up Level: flexible
Squeak Piggy
Class: 4 to 20 Space: yes Pace: wake up Level: flexible
The Blanket Game
Class: any Space: no Pace: calm Level: easy
True Or False
Class: any Space: no Pace: calm Level: easy
Truth Or Consequence
Class: 2 to 30 Space: no Pace: calm Level: flexible
Up Jenkins
Class: 6 to 15 Space: sit around a table Pace: wake up Level: easy
Very Large Class Choral Work
Class: any Space: no Pace: wake up Level: easy
What's the Time, Mr. Wolf?
Class: any Space: flexible Pace: variants Level: easy
Which One's Gone?
Class: 2 to 30 Space: in groups Pace: wake up Easy
Word Stress Chant & Spell
Class: any Space: no Pace: calm Level: easy
Zip Zap Vocabulary 1
Class: 6 to 30 Space: no Pace: wake up Level: easy
Zip Zap Vocabulary 2
Class: 6 to 20 Space: no Pace: wake up Level: easy

Step 4: More demanding speaking games

Once your pupils have a good grasp of the vocabulary or language structure, or with more advanced groups, try these alternative games:

All Change variant
Class: 6 to 50 Space: yes Pace: excitable Level: medium
Balls and Tenses

Class: Small group Space: a little Pace: Wake up Level: medium

Bang

Class: 2 to 20 Space: flexible Pace: wake up Level: flexible

Bogeyman

Class: 2 to 30 Space: flexible Pace: excitable Level: flexible

Brainstorm

Class: any Space: no Pace: wake up Level: any for vocabulary revision

British Bulldog

Class: 5 to 30 Space: yes Pace: excitable Level: flexible

Call My Bluff Grammar:

Class: any Space: no Pace: calm Level: flexible

Charades

Class: 2 to 20 Space: no Pace: calm Level: medium

Charades Race

Class: 2 to 30 Space: no Pace: calm Level: flexible

Chinese Whispers

Class: 3 up Space: no Pace: calm Level: flexible

Detective Game

Class: 6 to 30 Space: no Pace: calm Level: flexible

Dress Up Variant

Class: 4 to 30 Space: to dress up in Pace: wake up Level: medium

Fizz Buzz

Class: 4 to 24 Space: no Pace: calm Level: flexible

Flip A Card Class

Class: small group table top game Space: no Pace: calm Level: flexible

Guess the Word A

Class: 2 to 30 Space: no Pace: calm Level: flexible

Guess the Word B

Class: 2 to 40 Space: no Pace: calm Level: flexible

Hangman Variant

Class: pairs or small groups Space: no Pace: calm Level: harder, asking multiple questions

Happy Families

Class: table top game Space: sit in groups Pace: calm Level: easy

Hide & Seek Prepositions

Class: 2 to 30 Space: no Pace: calm Level: medium

Hot Potato variants

Class: any Space: no Pace: wake up Level: flexible

I Spy

Class: small group Space: no Pace: calm Level: easy

Keep A Straight Face

Class: 2 to 40 Space: no Pace: calm Level: flexible

Make a Sentence

Class: 2 to 30 Space: no Pace: calm Level: flexible

Name And Chase

Class: 2 to 30 Space: better with Pace: excitable Level: revision

One Up Stand Up

Class: 6 to 40 Space: no Pace: calm Level: flexible

Pass the Box

Class: 5 to 40 Space: flexible Pace: calm to wake up Level: flexible

Picture Flash Cards

Class: any Space: no Pace: flexible Level: flexible

Ping Pong

Class: 2 to 40 Space: no Pace: wake up Level: vocabulary revision

Potato Race

Class: 2 to 20 Space: yes, aisles OK Pace: excitable Level: easy

Preposition Challenge

Class: any in pairs Space: no Pace: calm Level: easy

Relay Race variant

Class: any Space: flexible Pace: wake up Level: medium

Sentence Conversion

Class: 2 to 30 Space: aisles Pace: wake up Level: flexible

Shop-A-Holics

Class: 5 to 30 Space: some Pace: wake up Level: easy

Simon Says

Class: any Space: no Pace: wake up Level: easy
Team Race Q & A shopping
Class: 2 to 30 Space: yes Pace: excitable Level: easy
Tongue Twisters
Class: any Space: no Pace: calm Level: medium
Treasure Hunt
Class: 2 to 40 Space: flexible Pace: calm - wake up Level: medium
What am I?
Class: 2 to 30 Space: no Pace: calm but can be noisy Level: medium
Who Wants to Be A Millionaire?
Class: 2 to 20 Space: no Pace: calm Level: flexible
Zambezi River
Class: 1 to 12 Space: aisles Pace: wake up Level: Easy

Step 5: Reading games

Many of the games in steps 1 to 4 can also be used with word flash cards to familiarise players with spelling. Here are some reading games that use word flashcards or texts:

Abracadanagram A
Class: 3 to 30 Space: no Pace: calm Level: flexible
Abracadanagram B
Class: 4 to large class Space: no Pace: calm Level: medium
All Change
Class: 6 to 20 Space: yes Pace: excitable Level: flexible
Balloon Fortunes
Class: 4 to 30 Space: aisles Pace: wake up Level: flexible
Bingo with words
Class: any Space: No Pace: calm Level: easy
Dancing Demons with words
Class: 3 to 21 Space: some Pace: wake up Level: easy
Find the Pairs B
Class: 2 to 40 Space: to sit in groups Pace: calm Level: easy

Jump the Line
Class: any Space: flexible Pace: wake up Level: easy
Ladders Basic
Class: 8 to 40 Space: yes Pace: excitable Level: easy
Musical Vocabulary
Class: 2 to 30 Space: yes Pace: wake up to excitable
Level: easy
Noughts & Crosses
Class: any in pairs Space: no Pace: calm Level: flexible
Quiz Race
Class: any Space: no Pace: calm Level: flexible
Rapid reaction
Class: 2 to 16 Space: circle Pace: wake up Level: easy
Reading Comprehension with a difference
Class: any Space: no Pace: calm Level: flexible
Reading Puzzle
Class: any Space: flexible Pace: calm Level: flexible
Remember & Write
Class: any Space: no Pace: calm Level: easy, remembering spelling of individual words
Show Me
Class: any Space: flexible Pace: wake up Level: easy
Silly Dialogues and Stories
Class: any Space: no Pace: calm Level: medium up
Team Race Listening
Class: 1 to 30 Space: yes Pace: excitable Level: easy
Tongue Twisters
Class: any Space: no Pace: calm Level: medium
Word Flash Cards
Class: 2 to 35 Space: no Pace: calm Level: easy
Zambezi River
Class: 1 to 12 Space: aisles Pace: wake up Level: easy

Step 6: Spelling and writing games

Abracadanagram B
Class: any Space: no Pace: calm Level: medium

Abracadanagram C
Class: any Space: no Pace: calm - wake up Level: flexible
Anagrams
Class: any Space: no Pace: flexible Level: flexible
Bingo A writing option
Class: any Space: no Pace: calm Level: easy
Bangle Game
Class: 6 to any size Space: no Pace: Lively Level: flexible
Boggle
Class: any Space: no Pace: calm Level: medium
Bucket Game
Class: any Space: no Pace: calm Level: flexible
Decoding
Class: any Space: no Pace: calm Level: easy
Figure It Out
Class: 2 to 30 Space: aisles OK Pace: wake up Level: medium
Hangman
Class: any Space: no Pace: calm Level: easy
Hidden Picture B
Class: 2 to 30 Space: optional Pace: calm Level: easy
Guess the word B
Class: 2 to 40 Space: no Pace: calm Level: easy
Make a sentence
Class: 2 to 30 Space: no Pace: calm Level: medium
Making up Stories
Class: 2 to 30 Space: no Pace: calm Level: medium
Match Up
Class: 6 to 40 Space: children circulate Pace: calm Level: easy
Mystery Bag
Class: 1 to 20 Space: no Pace: calm Level: easy
Ping Pong
Class: any Space: no Pace: wake up Level: vocabulary revision or drilling short sentences
Proverb Pairs
Class: any Space: no Pace: calm Level: medium
Question & Answer

Class: any Space: no Pace: calm Level: flexible

Q & A Lottery

Class: any Space: no Pace: calm Level: flexible

Quiz Race

Class: any Space: no Pace: calm Level: medium

Remember & Write

Class: any Space: no Pace: calm Level: easy

Shopping Memory

Class: any in groups Space: no Pace: calm Level: flexible

Silly Dialogues and Stories

Class: any Space: no Pace: calm Level: medium to difficult

Spell and Act

Class: 2 to 40 Space: no Pace: calm Level: easy

Spell and Speak

Class: 2 to 30 Space: no Pace: calm Level: medium

Spelling Board Game

Class: any Space: no Pace: calm Level: flexible

Spot the Difference

Class: any Space: no Pace: calm Level: medium

Stop

Class: 2 to 40 Space: no Pace: calm Level: flexible

The Big Freeze Spelling idea

Class: any Space: flexible Pace: calm Level: easy

Treasure Hunt

Class: 2 to 40 Space: no Pace: calm Level: medium

Vocab. Cut Outs

Class: any Space: no Pace: calm Level: flexible

Word Challenge

Class: any Space: no Pace: calm Level: flexible

Word Photographs

Class: any Space: no Pace: flexible Level: flexible

Write It Up

Class: 2 to 35 Space: no Pace: wake up Level: flexible

Writing Race

Class: 2 to 40 Space: aisles OK Pace: wake up
Level: flexible

Games ideal for specific grammar or vocabulary

99% of the games can be played to teach any grammar or vocabulary. Having said that certain games are ideal for specific language.

Actions

Step 1 Matching and Mirroring
Class: any Space: flexible Pace: wake up Level: flexible
Step 1 Copycat Commands
Class: any Space: no Pace: wake up Level: easy
Step 1 The Big Freeze
Class: any Space: flexible Pace: Calm Level: Easy
Step 2 Twister
Class: small groups Space: yes Pace: wake up Level: easy
Step 2 Simon Says
Class: any Space: no Pace: wake up Level: easy
Step 3 Miming Games
Class: 2 to 40 Space: flexible Pace: wake up Level: flexible

Alphabet

Step 2 Alphabet A
Class: 2 to 30 children in small groups or working alone
Space: no Pace: flexible Level: easy
Step 3 Jackpot
Class: 3 to 35 Space: no Pace: calm Level: easy
Step 3 Hangman
Class: 2 to small class Space: no Pace: calm Level: easy
Step 3 Zambezi River
Class: 1 to 35 Space: yes Pace: wake up Level: easy

See also all the numbers and counting games grouped under the letter C.

Body parts

Step 1 Matching and Mirroring
Class: any Space: no Pace: wake up Level: flexible
Step 1 Copycat Commands
Class: any Space: no Pace: wake up Level: easy
Step 1 Head to Head
Class: 4 to 30 Space: flexible Pace: excitable Level: easy
Step 2 Board Bash
Class: 2 to 30 Space: no Pace: calm Level: easy
Step 2 Twister
Class: small group Space yes Pace: wake up Level: easy
Step 2 Simon Says
Class: any Space: no Pace: wake up Level: easy
Step 3 Jungle Treasure
Class: 8 to 20 Space: yes Pace: wake up Level: flexible

Clothing

Step 1 Copycat Commands
Class: any Space: no Pace: wake up Level: easy
Step 2 Dress Up Race
Class: 4 to 30 Space: some Pace: wake up Level: easy
Step 2 Simon Says
Class: any Space: no Pace: wake up Level: flexible
Steps 2 and Three Colour Wolf
Class: any Space: yes Pace: excitable Level: easy
Step 2 Twister
Class: small group Space: yes Pace: wake up Level: easy
Step 3 or 4 Colour the Card
Class: pair work Space: no Pace: calm Level: easy
Step 4 Dress Up
Class: 2 to 30 Space: a little Pace: wake up Level: medium

Colours

Step 2 Twister

Class: small group Space: yes Pace: wake up Level: easy
Step 2 and 3 Colour Wolf
Class: any Space: yes Pace: excitable Level: easy
Step 3 or 4 Colour the Card
Class: pair work Space: no Pace: calm Level: easy

Comparatives

Step 3 or 4 Higher or Lower
Class: any Space: no Pace: calm Level: easy

Counting and numbers

Step 1 Count the Cards
Class: 2 to 30 Space: no Pace: wake up Level: easy
Step 2 Telephone Game
Class: 6 to 30 Space: no Pace: calm Level: easy
Step 3 Add up the Dice
Class: any Space: no Pace: calm Level: adding up
Step 3 Guess the Price
Class: any Space: no Pace: calm Level: flexible
Step 3 Pass the Ball
Class: 2 to 30 Space: flexible Pace: calm Level: easy
Step 3 Higher or Lower
Class: any Space: no Pace: calm Level: easy
Step 3 Zambezi River
Class: small groups Space: no Pace: Wake up Level: easy
Step 3 Jackpot
Class: 3 to 35 Space: no Pace: calm Level: easy
Step 3 One Lemon
Class: 4 to 35 Space: no Pace: Calm Level: easy
Step 4 Clap and Count
Class: 1 to 30 Space: no Pace: calm Level: easy
Step 4 How Many
Class: 2 to 40 Space: flexible Pace: wake up Level: flexible
Step 4 Match Stick Game

Class: small groups Space: children sit in groups Pace: calm
Level: easy adding up

Step 4 Don't Drop the Bomb
Class: 2 to 20 Space: yes Pace: excitable Level: easy

Step 4 Fizz Buzz
Class: small group Space: no Pace: calm Level: flexible

Directions

Step 2 Grandma's Directions
Class: any Space: aisles OK Pace: wake up Level: easy
Level: easy, following simple directions

Step 3 Directions on the Board
Class: any Space: no Pace: calm Level: easy

Step 4 Blind Directions
Class: 2 to 30 Space: flexible Pace: excitable Level: easy

Step 4 Elastic Band Game
Class: 3 to 30 Space: no Pace: calm Level: easy

Families

Step 3 or 4 Happy Families
Class: small group table top game Space: to sit in groups
Pace: calm Level: easy

Prepositions

Step 2 Where Is It?
Class: 2 to 30 Space: no Pace: calm Level: flexible

Step 3 Preposition Mimes
Class: Any Space: aisles Pace: wake up Level: easy

Step 4 Hide and Seek Prepositions
Class: 2 to 30 Space: flexible Pace: wake up
Level: easy, making sentences

Step 4 Preposition Challenge
Class: any, in pairs Space: no Pace: calm Level: easy

Pronunciation and Phonemes

See a series of games grouped under the letter P including: Phonemes – Wall Charts, Pronunciation Chart Game, Pronunciation Game, Pronunciation Hands Up, Phoneme Race, Phonemes Hangman, Pronunciation Pictures, Pronunciation Word Stress and Word Stress Chant and Spell.

Telling the Time

What's the Time, Mr. Wolf?
Class: any Space: flexible Pace: flexible Level: easy

Question and answer games

Step 1 or 3 True or False
Class: any Space: no Pace: calm Level: easy
Step 2 Question and Answer
Class: any Space: no Pace: wake up Level: easy
Step 3 Ladders Q and A
Class: 8 to 40 Space: yes Pace: excitable Level: easy
Step 3 Scissors Paper Stone
Class: 2 to 40 Space: class stand in two lines Pace: calm Level: easy
Step 3 Team Race Q and A
Class: 3 to 30 Space: yes Pace: excitable Level: easy
Step 3 Relay Race
Class: any Space: aisles OK Pace: wake up Level: easy
Step 3 Joker
Class: small group Space: to sit in group Pace: calm Level: easy
Step 3 Up Jenkins
Class: 6 to 15 Space: seating around table Pace: wake Up Level: easy to lower intermediate
Steps 3 or 4 Find Your Friend
Class: 6 to 40 Space: aisles OK Pace: calm Level: easy
Step 4 Potato Race

Class: 2 to 30 Space: yes, aisles OK Pace: excitable
Level: easy, asking and answering questions drill
Step 5 or 6 Quiz Race
Class: any Space: no Pace: calm Level: flexible

Short dialogues

Step 3 Scissors Paper Stone
Class: 2 to 40 Space: aisles OK Pace: calm Level: easy
Step 3 British Bulldog
Class: 5 to 30 Space: yes Pace: excitable Level: easy
Step 4 Bogeyman
Class: 2 to 30 Space: flexible Pace: excitable Level: flexible
Step 4 What Am I?
Class: 2 to 30 Space: no Pace: calm Level: medium
Step 6 Silly Dialogues
Class: Any Space: no Pace: calm Level: flexible

Games ideal for playing with songs or rhymes

A few games in this book are ideal for use with music.

Step 1: The Big Freeze, Musical Vocabulary
Step 3: Duck, Duck Goose, Oranges, Pass the Parcel, Piggy in the Middle
Step 4: Hot Potato, Limbo

If you are keen on using music in class then you may like my songs activity book that comes with the Teaching English Songs 1 CD – available on CD or download as preferred from:
www.teachingenglishgames.com/eslsongs.htm

Games to use with teens or adults

There is a separate book available for teens and adults with drills, fluency based speaking activities and more advanced ideas: www.teachingenglishgames.com/esl-for-adults.

From this book the following games are suitable:

Listening:

All Change (some may perceive as childish), Abracadanagram, Bingo, Rapid Reaction, Show Me, True or False, Simon Says – harder version, Team Race on the Board, Where Is It?

Speaking:

Alphabet B, Balls and Tenses, Charades, Chinese Whispers with tongue twisters or proverbs, Blind Directions, Brainstorm, Detective Game, Find the Pairs, Find your Friend, Fizz Buzz, Guess the Action, Guess the Word, Hangman, Happy Families, Hidden Picture, Hide and Seek Prepositions, Hot Potato, Make a Sentence, Match Up, Mystery Bag, Noughts and Crosses, Pass the Pictures, Phoneme Hangman, Pictionary, Ping Pong, Pronunciation Chart Game, Pronunciation Game, Pronunciation Hands Up, Proverb Pairs, Rapid Reaction, Relay Race and advanced variant, Scissors Paper Stone, Sentence Conversion, Shopping List Memory Game, Spoon Game, True or False 2 without the blanket, What's the Time Mr. Wolf? What am I? Which one's gone? Zip Zap vocab revision

Reading:

Abracadanagram, Bingo, Find the Pairs, Reading Puzzle, Proverb Pairs, Rapid Reaction, Remember and Write, Riddle Pairs, Show Me, Word Flash Cards

Writing (mostly spelling games):

Abracadanagram, Anagrams, Boggle, Figure it Out, Hangman, Guess the Word, Make a Sentence, Match Up, Ping Pong, Remember and Write, Shopping List Memory Game, Stop, Treasure Hunt, Word Challenge, Writing Race.

TIPS ON USING THE GAMES

It is possible to teach a whole lesson with games or pepper your class with them in between using the textbook or other activities.

(1) The category

Each game has a category. There is the listening category of games, which are for introducing new vocabulary, new grammar and also for revision. Next is the speaking category. These games involve various degrees of difficulty, from limited drills to freer speaking games. Occasionally the speaking opportunity is just saying a rhyme as part of a game. Most games lend themselves to learning any vocabulary or grammar. The listening and speaking categories make up the bulk of the games on the basis that this is what is missing most in classes today. Some reading, writing, spelling and pronunciation games are also included, and they usually combine one or more of the other skills.

(2) Group size

All the games in this book are suitable for small groups of up to 20 children. However many games have variants for use with large classes. There are even games that work with a lecture hall of 80 students on benches. Equally if you are tutoring any private pupils many games can be adapted, although I have also written a dedicated resource for one to one.

The detailed index indicates the ideal class size for each game. Many teachers successfully use these games with more pupils than specified in the ideal group size. However be mindful of a game dragging due to too much waiting time. There is nothing worse than becoming bored sitting around waiting for a turn when there are too many players, and each turn takes too long.

Look for the variants to suit different class sizes in the game descriptions.

(3) Level

The level indicated for each game is often flexible because the games can be adapted in so many ways. For a beginner introduce fewer words and use simpler structures. The quantity or complexity of the language chosen by the teacher dictates the level while the rules of the game remain the same.

It should be noted that there is no link between the level and the recommended age. Advanced games are not for older children; they can be played with younger children who are at that level. Equally adults can enjoy and learn from some of the beginner games. Most of the games provided are for beginner to intermediate levels because in most schools where children are being taught English as a second language, these are the most relevant. However a teacher may use basic games to drill advanced grammar. My teen/adult games book is available for higher levels.

(4) Materials

Picture flashcards are essential for most of the games. Either buy some ready-made, make your own or have your class draw pictures on card and laminate them so that they last. I have a cute set for sale in download here:

www.teachingenglishgames.com/eslflashcards

It is a good idea to use real items or toys with younger children. You might want to ask the class to bring things in, though that requires supervision. Over time build up a collection of props from car boot or garage sales, charity shops and markets. For example enhance a lesson on the present continuous by using old clothing for the dressing up games in this book. Using real objects adds novelty, helps tactile learners and makes the lesson seem more relevant to real life.

Many of the games require no materials or have a variant using no materials, aside from the class board. These can be especially useful if you have a few minutes spare at the end of your lesson or if you are waiting for people to arrive who are late.

(5) Age

All games are suitable for children aged 6-12 and many for children aged 4-5. A list of games also suitable for adults is included at the end of the detailed index. The games themselves are simple as far as learning the rules. Some games have variants for older or younger children. The trick is to have an alternative on standby and be ready to simplify the language if a game is not working well.

Specialist resources by the author are available for children aged 3-6 and for teens and adults on:

www.teachingenglishgames.com and on Amazon.

(6) Pace

Games are labelled according to pace: excitable, wake up and calm. Use these categories strategically to control the energy level in your group. For example if your class comes right after a lesson with a deathly dull teacher, who sends all the children into total lethargy, then start with a lively game to wake every one up. If your class is immediately after the recreation period you might start with a calming game. I recommend excitable games for nearer the end of the lesson, but always calm the children down before sending them out of the classroom so the teacher after you does not have to deal with a riot!

It is possible to teach the whole lesson with games, however the likelihood is that you will have course books to work through. Follow the book using games to teach the vocabulary and grammar in each unit. You may be in the habit of opening up the textbook the minute you walk into class and having pupils take turns in reading from it out loud. Instead use listening games to first introduce the vocabulary and language structures in the text, reinforce it with further listening or speaking games, and then open the book. Students will now get more out of the unit because they will understand it. Reading will now serve to reinforce the newly acquired vocabulary and language.

Even if you adhere to the most traditional methods, you can still use games here and there during the lesson to keep the pupils focused and alert.

(7) Competition

Avoid competition with children younger than six. By all means play against the clock and have races with youngsters, but everybody wins, not just the child finishing first. Make sure young children always succeed at the task in the given time frame and stretch it if necessary. In particular, with younger players below age 7, let the game go on until all the teams or people have completed. Young children can burst into tears from the pain of failure at what seems a trifle to adults, so set the game up for everyone to complete successfully.

An element of competition with children over six definitely gives an edge to games and children are often more motivated to make an effort to remember words if points are at stake. In order to ensure a variety of winners and a bonding of the whole class mix up your groups, sometimes putting all the bright kids together and sometimes allocating the best children to be team leaders. Having competing teams spreads out the winning and losing. Individual students within a team are accountable and have a responsibility towards their team.

A teacher may freely rig the play in order to keep scores as close together as possible and avoid having one team or group trailing way behind the others. Do this by giving easier questions to the worst students. Be subtle since you don't want anyone to notice.

While some competition livens things up a bit, one doesn't want to make every game a point scoring exercise. There is no need to make a big deal about who wins, after all it is the learning that is important, not who wins the game, unless you want to specifically praise a certain student because he or she needs extra encouragement.

(8) Mixed abilities

In any group one always has children of different natural abilities and one of the teacher's greatest challenges is to stretch the brighter children, while nurturing the less gifted ones. Using games allows for this beautifully, as long as the teacher creates a balance between competition and team spirit. If there is too much competition then weaker students, who always lose, will quickly become demotivated. Whereas team spirit can be created by allowing students to help each other, and not just within a team, but within the whole class. More academic children can stretch themselves by helping the slower ones.

Games allow you to make the most of your brightest children. For example, let the most talented children work together initially, and once they have learned the material, send them out as group leaders to the rest of the class, to lead a series of games, or use them as referees or runners in the games for quality control. This will be mentioned in the instructions for certain games. Of course you have to let them play too sometimes!

Never crush or ignore a bright student. You may have a bilingual child in your class. Don't feel threatened! Use that child to help you with pronunciation, with checking errors in group games, as a team leader, as a demonstrator and to write things on the board for you.

(9) Logistics

There are enough options and adaptations to allow you to play most of the games in this book, whether or not your classroom is cramped. Consider going outside or to the gym once in a while, to play games that need a big space, perhaps for an end of term lesson.

Watch out for obstacles in the classroom if pupils are coming up to the board or moving around. Make sure all school bags are placed out of the way. Replace running with fast walking for greater safety and also to control the class more easily.

(9a) Forming teams

To quickly create teams of 12 count in unison with the class from 1-12, pointing at a different student on each number. Those students are all in team A. Pupils should make a note of their team letter as a precaution. Then count the next batch who become the Bs, again counting up with the class. Keep those teams for the whole lesson. If you notice one team always wins swap over some of the talented pupils. Vary how you form the teams by counting across the rows, vertically or by dividing the class up into imaginary squares. This way your pupils are always in different teams. When pupils are expert at counting from 1-12 make up your teams by counting from 13 upwards.

The size of your teams will depend on how many you have in your class and how many teams you want. Fewer teams can be easier to manage.

(9b) Giving each member of the class a number

You may sometimes want to give each pupil a number so that all the number 1s can do one thing, all the number 2s do another and so on. You want to do this quickly but in a way that the students will remember the number they are given. First instruct pupils to write down their number as soon as they are given it so as not to forget it. Then the whole class counts with you. Point at the first child on 1. He or she becomes number 1. Point at the second child on 2, and so on. When pupils come to their own number they place their hand on their chest as they say their number and then write it down.

In this way you quickly organise your class for a game while everyone drills counting together, but counting with a purpose, not just meaningless repetition. Use this method to practise different numbers. Count from 113 to 122 instead of the usual 1 to 10 or count backwards. Use the alphabet instead of numbers for variety.

(10)Team slogans

Divide the class into groups and let each group identify itself with a name such as an animal. Give each group a chant or slogan to perform standing up with actions or clapping. The groups can be asked to say their slogan when they win a team game as a reward, or for fun to break up a period of sitting.

Let children create their own slogans in teams. Make sure the slogans are correct grammatically before being voted as the official slogan for that team. If you have beginners use simple slogans such as "We are the birds and we love to fly, we are the birds and we fly up high!" If that is too difficult start with "We are the birds, we are the birds!" Let groups add more to their slogans later in the term as they progress.

(11) Classroom Management and Noise

It is vital to keep discipline in class so that time is well spent. Most of keeping good order comes from the teacher's attitude. Just because a teacher uses classroom games does not mean an excuse for a party.

(11a) Some essential basics to manage a class

☺Together with your pupils define the rules in the first lesson and post them on a classroom wall for reference. Knowing WHY a rule is in place makes it easier to keep. You must establish the rules on day one and stick to them! This really works, as the teacher below testifies: 'I want to share a classroom management idea that works for me. I am an early childhood teacher and on the first day of school I sit with my students in a circle. I ask the children to make the rules that they would like to follow and I post those rules right next to the calendar. Whenever a rule is not followed I go back to the poster and ask the misbehaving child to follow the rule next time and tell the other children to remind him/her. I have no reward and no punishment in my classroom. The responsibility is with the children and they feel very powerful.'

☺Be consistent in applying your rules. If you are arbitrary about how you dish out your rewards and 'consequences' or punishments, you will undermine the rules themselves.

☺Praise good behaviour to generate love and self-esteem. Whatever you do, avoid being like so many parents who spend their time telling their children, "don't do this", and "don't do that". By focusing on the positive in order to draw more attention to it you may attract more of what you focus on. Reward and appreciate good behaviour. Happy faces work well and cost nothing as this teacher describes:

'Write the children's names on the board and tell them there will be a prize for the child with the most 'happy faces' at the end of the class. The first time the class gets rowdy, without saying anything, draw a happy face next to a quiet child's name. This will instantly get the attention of the class and I have found that if you give the rowdiest child a happy face the instant he or she behaves better (even if only slightly better), then he or she will make an effort for the rest of the class.'

Often children who are rowdy are used to being left out of privileges so won't bother making an effort to behave. So if you recognise good behaviour from them quickly and acknowledge it, they will be quick to try and take part.

Here is an extended version of the 'happy face' principle shared by a teacher:

'I have prepared a motivation chart for the entire class, one for boys and one for girls as all the names cannot fit in one. The names are in the left column and the parameters for which I expect an improvement are:

1. General class behaviour,
2. Regularity in class work and homework,
3. Contribution to class either by giving ideas or getting some interesting facts and sharing or creating/finding a piece of art and putting it up on the class bulletin board,
4. Novelty - anything new and creative that is done by the child purely on self-motivation and
5. Personal cleanliness (clean shoes, ironed clothes, nails trimmed and hygiene).

These 5 points form the five columns. There is one row for the whole class too.

There are no black marks. Only red stars are given as rewards. This does not mean that whenever the child completes his or her homework on time, she will get red star. It is customized and subjective depending on the effort that child must have taken to complete it on time. When a naughty boy stays quiet for a period, he gets a red star while the others don't. A brilliant student who contributes to class and shares knowledge will earn a red star in that column.

I have found this chart works wonders improving the behaviour of my classes of 10 year olds. With warm regards, Lalithashree.'

☺If you are part of a school, know the law and rules of your institution before you go into the classroom for the first time, and work in harmony with the school. Start out strict and fair - and stay that way! Being strict is not about looking stern and being bossy. It is about making sure the rules are kept, in a firm but fair way. It's possible to be a fun, loving teacher and be strict with your class at the same time.

☺A prize for good behaviour could be a round of applause from the whole class or being given a special task by the teacher such as leading a game or writing something up on the board.

☺Don't break your own rules by raising your voice to be heard. Instead talk quietly or stop and wait. Your class should know that for every minute you are kept waiting they will receive extra English homework, or whatever consequence you have designated.

☺Children love the sound of their own name more than anything else so use an individual's name for praise and avoid using it when telling someone off.

☺Conversely have a student write the names of everyone in class on the board at the start of the lesson and when a student is naughty erase a letter from his or her name. The kids hate that! When that child behaves better add back the letter.

☺Create teams and deduct or reward points to a team's score during a game for good behaviour. Your class will respond naturally by using peer pressure to keep the naughty children from misbehaving.

☺Empower your children with choices. For example, ask a naughty child, "Do you want me to speak to your Dad or would you like to listen to the class?" By asking a question you give the child the power to choose, whereas if you use a threat such as, "I'll call your Dad if you don't behave", you take the initiative away and seem tyrannical. For example try, "You can either play the game properly or you can sit in the corner, which do you choose?" The child will probably choose to play the game properly, and you have made them responsible for their behaviour.

☺Society is constantly evolving and every individual has the choice to move with the times or remain the same. Where before a teacher might have administered a good slap, yelled at a student or handed out a punishment directly, now teachers and parents are using 'non-violent communication' techniques. I can highly recommend becoming familiar with these.

☺Prevention is better than cure, so try giving boisterous children an important task *before* they start to play up. They may respond well to the responsibility.

☺With a large class it is especially important to hand things out quickly or use a system to have this done, such as giving the well-behaved children the task as a reward. Sing a song together or do some counting to occupy the class while materials are handed out.

☺Play a mystery game. Before you start an activity, say that you will be watching the whole class for 3 well-behaved children who will be rewarded.

☺Keep the pace of a game moving so children do not have time to mess around as if they do they will miss something, not score a point or miss a turn.

☺Follow noisy games with quiet games or a worksheet to keep a lid on the level of excitement. If you are feeling cautious, use the calm games only. Pepper your classes with 5-minute games in between textbook exercises.

☺Most listening games can be played in silence so it is wrong to assume that using games automatically means more noise in class.

☺Only play games where you know you can keep a handle on the situation. For example there is no point playing a boisterous game with a lot of movement with more than around 20 children. With large classes, including classes of up to 60 children, you need games where the children have limited movement, such as standing up, sitting down or making gestures while remaining in their seats.

(11b) Attention grabbers

☺Start an English song the children know and love. They will all join in with you and at the end you'll have their attention.

☺Clap out a pattern, which the class must clap back. Keep going until all the children have joined in.

☺Start a rhyme students know with actions.

☺Use quiet cues such as heads down or lights off. Vary these with other quiet cues such as "Give me five". 1--sit down; 2--hands folded in your lap; 3--face the speaker; 4--eyes and ears open; 5--mouths closed. Teach this repeatedly in the first lessons and after a few weeks, you only have to say "Give me five: 1, 2, 3, 4, 5", and the children will do it.

☺From teacher Kashmira Vazifdar: "Your tips on class management do wonders. I have been using the give me a 5 technique for several years and it truly is effective. Another technique I use when I have a noisy class on is to do various hand and head actions. I start any action like a wave, a flying bird, or just hands swaying from side to side, and the class copies me till we reach the last action of the hands placed lightly over the mouth, which has been established as an action for silence. The entire class is then silent, attentive, energised and focused to begin the class on a quiet note."

☺The Magic 1 2 3 idea also works well. When a child does not comply start counting 1, 2... The child knows that if you get to 3 there will be some sort of consequence, such as missing out on the next game. If you use this and you reach 3, you must follow through with an appropriate consequence consistently.

☺Play the game Sit and Be Silent from this book.

(11c) Loud individuals

If you have trouble with a few children who always shout out the answer before others be careful not to kill their enthusiasm by crushing them. Speak to them privately, explaining that everyone should have a turn. Pick children out to answer in alphabetical order or draw names out of a hat to be fair. Rather than asking children to put their hands up to answer a question pull a name out of the hat. This avoids wasting valuable minutes while the whole class strain and go "ooh teacher, please sir!!!" etc. When you can only pick one child out of sixty you want to spend as much time on task and as little time as possible on logistics. Still it is good to use variety and having the children put their hands up to answer does get them to move their bodies a little. In general you want to try and avoid having only one child involved in an activity while the other sixty watch. Use the games in this book where at least a handful of children participate at once.

(11d) Summary

In summary, establish the rules and consequences for good and bad behaviour, apply them consistently, set a good example, use peer pressure and points, and use attention-grabbing cues. Above all play suitable games where you know you can keep in control of your class. If you cannot manage your class you should realize that, although it sounds harsh to say so, you are wasting your pupils' time.

(12) Movement

Aristotle said that the three things children should concentrate on are music, arithmetic and physical education. Arithmetic develops the mind, music the emotions and physical education the body. Nowadays we have a broader curriculum but nonetheless children benefit from being active. You have surely noticed how most children like to run everywhere. Children generally do not walk; they skip, hop, run and naturally can't keep still. These days we coop children up in classrooms like battery hens and it is not natural, it's not natural for the hens either for that matter.

If you include movement in your language classes you will get better results. Movement will snap the children out of any lethargy or boredom that they may be in as a result of sitting for long periods. Children often switch classrooms for different lessons and that is good, but I maintain that using movement during the class gives better results than keeping children still.

If you have space then using movement is easy. If not just have the children stand up, sit down, move various body parts, point to a different picture around the room or pass things around in the context of a game. Bring different children up to the front of the class and have others distribute things for you or collect them in. The games in this book give many ways of including movement, even with very large classes.

(13) Group work

Always demonstrate with a group first so everyone is clear on what is to be done.

Tell children to use whispering or quiet talking to keep the overall noise level down.

Use a signal, such as flicking the lights off and on. On the signal the children know the group time is over and that they must be silent immediately.

To play a small group game when you have too large a class, sub-divide. Make up a small central group for the game while the others do a written task. When a child in the group has spoken once or twice he or she goes back to the main group and someone from the main group comes in to the sub-group. For example 12 children are passing two balls around saying sentences or words. When a child has had the ball twice his turn is up and someone takes his place. This has to happen seamlessly without stopping the game so you keep up the pace and flow of children through the game.

Very large classes: If you are able to divide the class up have one group on school computers doing worksheets or word games, or even homework which they can email to you. Another group can be doing something on the board, another on the overhead projector, another can be watching a video or doing a listening comprehension. In this way you have only a few groups engaged in speaking while the rest are involved in quiet activities. Rotate so each group has a turn at everything. Your overall noise level will be manageable this way.

Let each group create a poster with words they know and take turns showing the class and naming the items. For more advanced students use this idea to make up and present stories, jokes, funny things that happened, favourite films and why, and so on. Each group can also create a newsletter, or take it in turns to do so. This can be posted in the class for the week for everyone to read.

(14) Pair work

Role-plays are excellent for speaking fluency. Demonstrate up front first and then let the class work in pairs. Allow only whispering to keep the overall noise down. Any pairs caught using the native language instead of English risk losing a point or being disqualified, or whatever measures you are using to maintain discipline and productive work.

(15) Spoon-fed choral repetition

When a teacher has a huge class of 45 students or more – even up to 120 – this can seem like the only option to get children speaking English. However it is dull and not particularly effective, although it is better than never letting the children say anything!

If you have to use this, use it sparingly. Instead look for ideas in the games that follow. Rather than making the children repeat things back like parrots why not put the vocabulary and grammar you are teaching into rhymes or songs. Let the children make up a rhyme for homework, with a given words or a specific sentence in it. Once you have a few decent contributions the class can learn those for fun. At least the children feel they are being creative and thinking about the language rather than just mindlessly repeating back what they hear from you.

(16) Worksheets

Large classes may mean that giving out worksheets is expensive and wasteful. Ideas are to give out one worksheet per group of children and let them copy it, or display it on an overhead projector. Laminate worksheets which children fill in with washable pens so they can be wiped and reused over and over again.

(17) Getting to know the children

Have children wear nametags in class to start with. While it may be a sea of faces at first gradually you will get to know them all.

To learn names quickly associate a feature with the name such as Lisa with the glasses, pouting Lena or blue-eyed Joe. Obviously you keep the feature to yourself but this helps you match the name to the person.

If you participate in school events and at lunch the children will see more of you and this will help you learn their names and get to know them.

They will appreciate it if you show an interest in them as to their likes and dislikes and who they are outside of class. If it is possible for you then invite groups of children back to your house for a drink to watch a cartoon or for a board game.

If possible allow a few minutes of class time for individuals to come and see you with requests for help while the rest of the class are occupied with something. You may not have time to explain everything but do note down any requests and cover them again in future classes.

(18) Karaoke

Bear in mind that just because you may be a closet opera singer does not mean all your students will enjoy singing. Most will, but for some it could be an excruciating experience. Therefore never make it obligatory and allow students to speak words in time to the music instead if preferred. Older boys will probably not enjoy singing but usually both sexes of younger children will love it.

If there is a budget available then a Karaoke machine could be one of your best investments although you may download and play karaoke tracks from a computer which children sing along to. If playing music from a computer please, please get some decent portable speakers! Let children learn songs in groups if group work is feasible for you, or as a class if not. Teach the vocabulary in the songs first using games and ask children to write down the lyrics and learn a verse at a time for homework. Let the children give you their suggestions for actions to the song so you have some movement too. If you have several classes at the end of term let each class perform to the others.

(19) Performances for motivation

Many children love to show off and perform. If you have several classes put on a show where pupils perform to each other. Things to perform can be songs, rhymes, mimes, role-plays, question and answer type quizzes, vocabulary quizzes, or drawing pictures according to instructions. Even without the combined class show you can run friendly performances in an effort to focus the children and motivate them to concentrate when practising together in groups before showing the class.

(20)Teaching One to One Tips

For those teaching children one to one, or in pairs then I recommend that you consult the webpage below where you will find a demonstration video and games adapted for one to one teaching. www.teachingenglishgames.com/how-to-teach-a-child-to-speak-english

(21) Short plays are ideal for small groups

If you have the good fortune to teach children in small groups then plays and skits are ideal. Putting on short plays for parents or friends is a highly motivating activity. Many children absolutely love attention and showing off what they have learned. A script should be simple and repetitive, and preferably with a funny twist. This will give a great deal of pleasure to the child, who will be happy to rehearse and perform. The parents will be so impressed with your results that they will be sure to continue sending their child to the lessons. You will find easy, fun short plays that are ideal for beginners here:

www.teachingenglishgames.com/eslplays.htm.

(22) Adding value to enhance your teaching and reputation

To help your students beyond the classroom lend or recommend children's films, with an English soundtrack and possibly subtitles in the native language so that the children will actually watch the movies! Your pupils will watch these many times over willingly and absorb a huge amount of language subconsciously.

Buy them second hand online or locally, at charity shops or boot fairs (garage sales). Over time build up a library of these for your teaching purposes.

You could also build a library of comic books to lend. You would not expect your students to understand all that much text initially but the pictures tell the story and the subconscious will be absorbing the language all the time. You might want to take a deposit from students on loan of your material to ensure its return.

(23) Summary of top tips:

☺Always start with games from step 1 - you cannot expect the children to be able to play games with the language until they understand it. Steps 1 and 2 are vital.

☺Follow the natural learning process of 1.listening, 2.speaking, 3.reading and 4.writing. Use the detailed index to select games from each step.

☺Use games intermittently throughout your class in combination with your course work, to reinforce or to prepare for it.

☺Mix in calm, wake up and excitable games to keep your class alert and on their toes, and use movement games every now and then. Note that in some games, movement can be used even while the class remain seated.

☺Start easy, build confidence and make it harder gradually. This applies to the level of language presented, the amount, and also the nature of the task according to the age of your pupils. Always make it easy to start with so everyone can do it, feels good about it and can therefore build on a solid foundation.

☺Be organised and ready with materials to keep momentum going so the children do not have time to get bored.

☺Cultivate team spirit and use competition for the purpose of keeping everyone motivated rather than as an end in itself. Avoid competition with youngsters under 7.

☺Use resources that you have to hand such as props in the classroom, clothing, body parts and furniture around you. Have children make picture and word flashcards for you if you do not have any.

☺Keep an eye on the games you choose so that children are not sitting around waiting for their turn.

☺Always have reserve material and be ready to switch to another game immediately if something is not working.

☺Always stop the games while they are going well and children are still enjoying them.

☺Use short games for revision frequently and revise previous themes covered often. Pupils can revise a whole theme in a few minutes with a game. Repetition is the mother of skill.

☺Surprise your pupils by avoiding a predictable routine.

☺Use masses of praise and encouragement.

☺Use the class talent to help you. A bilingual student in your class, who may speak better English than the teacher, is a blessing not a curse.

☺Speak to students in English as much as possible, using mime and demonstrations where possible rather than reverting to the native tongue. If you are teaching a multi-lingual class you will be used to doing this anyway.

☺Give tests at well-chosen moments so that even the children who usually do not do well have the pleasure of going home and telling their parents they got 9 or 10 out of 10.

☺Enjoy yourself!

GAMES A-B

Abracadanagram A

Category: Listening and reading variant
Group size: Best for small classes
Level: All levels
Materials: Picture or word flashcards
Age: 6 to 12
Pace: Wake up if using movement. Calm if children work individually at desks

How to play

This game is adaptable for different levels and ages. Divide the class into groups of three and give each group a pile of pictures and /or word flash cards to make sentences or questions from. Each player takes a flashcard. Call out a sentence such as "Jacky loves chocolate" and the three players must stand in the right order, to represent the sentence, holding their pictures up for the class to see.

A rule where the children cannot swap flashcards with each other but must switch places forces them to move, which helps learning. If your pupils cannot move then they will have to swap cards with each other until they are in the correct order.

With a big class recruit a couple of "runners" from your best students, who will have the job of going around and checking everyone has their pictures in the right order. Mix up picture and word flashcards for older players.

For variety have teams race each other to get into the correct order, calling out "Abracadanagram!" ready, at which point you or your runners check the sentence. The emphasis is always on completing rather than winning.

Language ideas

Here are ways of adapting the game to suit different levels with the sentence, "The cat sat on the mat" as an example: Young beginners: use only 2 pictures, a cat and a mat. Up a level: use 2 pictures, a cat and a mat combined with the words "the, sat, on" and "the".

For more advanced players use sentences with clauses, such as, "The cat sat on the mat, which was in the hallway, where the dog also slept under the stairs".

Use this game to reinforce grammatical structures, verb tenses or question forms.

Reading variant

To make it harder, give out a pile of words to each group but do not call out the sentence. Each group figures it out. You could also give a complete set of words to each group and ask them to form a question or statement from the words provided as fast as possible, not necessarily using all the words. The first few teams to form a correct sentence or question get a point for that round.

For example if you give out the following words: "do, does, you, he, she, they, like, likes, pizza" and a flashcard with "?" pupils can make a variety of questions and statements for drilling present tense and present tense question forms.

Materials

Use flashcards. Picture flashcards help with vocabulary retention. Word flashcards help with spelling. If you think it is too much work getting material together then simply use word flash cards, which your class can write out for you by copying the words off the board - one word per piece of paper. On the other hand colourful pictures make the task visually appealing and this will help dyslexic students and those who learn well from visuals.

Abracadanagram B

Category: Speaking and optional writing
Group size: 4 to 30 in small groups and large class variant
Level: All levels
Materials: Picture or word flashcards or the board
Age: 6 to 12
Pace: Wake up

Class organisation

Divide your class into small teams of 4 players each or into pairs. The fewer people per team the less chance some players will be distracted and not make any effort to join in. It is also highly desirable to have the teams swap around to avoid the same groups forming all the time, and the same people winning all the time.

How to play

On the word "Go!" one player from each team comes up to the front and collects picture flashcards and / or words for a sentence. The player dashes back to his or her team (preferably without cracking his or her skull on a desk corner because he or she is over-excited) and holds up each picture in turn. The team name the pictures and read out the words. Each player takes at least one card and together as a group the team creates a sentence out of the pictures and words given. When finished pupils call out

"Abracadanagram", or "Finished!" and you (or one of your runners, (see Abracadanagram A) go over and check that the sentence is correct. The team must read the sentence out loud. If you want to reinforce the sentence structure even more, have each team member write the sentence out before calling out "Finished". The team leader then brings that to you for checking.

At the end of round one another player from each team comes up to the front, returns the first set of flashcards and takes a second set back to the group. Alternatively if using different sentences for each team, players pass their words and pictures to the team next door.

Writing option

Make up a simple story using the vocabulary or grammar that you wish to reinforce. Split this story into sections and play Abracadanagram B as described above. On completion of each sentence the team writes it down and swaps cards with another team until all sentences have been unraveled. Now the teams race to put the sentences of the story in order through reading.

Material

Zip lock bags are useful to store picture and word flashcards. Alternatively dispense with all the material by writing up the words in a jumble on the board. The class, working as individuals or pairs, unscramble the sentences as fast as you write them up with pen and paper at their desks. This is not as fun as actually handling flashcards, which appeals to the often-neglected kinaesthetic and tactile learning style.

Large class variant

Divide the class into teams. Using your target structure ask pupils to each think of three sentences, or questions, and write them out in a jumble. It is helpful to have examples on the board, as you want your pupils' sentences to be accurate. If they are full of mistakes it will be very difficult to decipher them.

On your command pupils fold their paper in two and hand it to their team leader. Team leaders swap over all the papers with another team. If your class are on long benches and no one can move, have all papers collected at one end of the bench, and then passed forward one row. Take the front row and give it to the back. Papers are handed out again but only unfolded when you give the signal. Then everyone races to decipher the sentences they have been given.

While the class are silently deciphering their papers those who have worked out a sentence can put their hand up and read it out. This allows you to do a quality control check that way to see that most people are using the target language correctly. The first ten people win points for their respective teams.

Abracadanagram C

Category: Pair work speaking
Group size: Any class size including very large classes
Level: All levels
Materials: Picture or word flashcards, or the board
Age: 6 to 12
Pace: Wake up

Give your students a written task to complete, such as a crossword, while you prepare the board. Using the target structure and vocabulary write up a series of jumbled questions under letter A with jumbled answers under letter B. For example:

A	B
you how old are?	years am seven old I
name your is what?	Shelley name my is

Tell pupils to form pairs. One person is A. The other is B. On the word "go" the As work out their question and the Bs work out their answer. A then asks B the question and B answers. When a pair has finished your list they stand up. Wait until a few pairs are standing and then hear some of the questions and answers.

You don't have to use a question and answer format, but can use only questions, or only sentences. The sentences should be repetitive if you are drilling a certain structure. Throw in a few sentences which revise what you have been teaching in recent weeks.

If students get distracted during pair work, give a time limit for the task so everyone who finishes in the given time wins. If possible allow the pupils who struggle the most to sit next to the best students and allow copying so students may learn from each other!

Action Race

Category: Easy speaking - repeating words or short phrases
Group size: 2 to 40. Space needed down the aisles of the class
Level: Beginner
Materials: None
Age: 4 to 10
Pace: Wake up to Excitable

Put children in teams. With 30 children have five teams to limit waiting time. Place one chair per team at the front of the class with one student from each team in each chair. Call out an action and the children in the chairs do that action down to the end of the class and back to their seat.

Have the children name the action repeatedly as they move. For example they repeat "I am jumping" continuously as they jump down the class, only stopping when they reach their seats. You may award points for saying the English nicely as well as reaching the seat first. Watch out for children hurting themselves when trying to race. If in doubt do not play the game as a race. With 4 to 6 year olds avoid any kind of competition - all children succeed simply by completing the action.

Use this to work on any language. Repeat any given phrase continuously while hopping or jumping down the room. For 6 year olds and upwards the children only move when they are speaking since that prevents children from rushing down the classroom without saying anything.

All Change

Category: Listening, speaking and reading variants
Group size: Small groups of 6 to 20
Level: Beginner to Intermediate
Materials: Picture or word flashcards
Age: 4 to 12
Pace: Excitable

How to play

Players stand in a circle with one player in the middle. Each player in the circle has a picture or word flash card. Call out two of the picture card items. The two players holding these cards have to change places without the person in the middle taking one of their spots in the circle. When the person in the middle succeeds in taking a place in the circle, the other player hands over his or her card and takes a turn in the middle. At any time call out "All change!" and this means that everyone has to change places. Use this if you see someone is getting stuck in the middle.

Language ideas

Either name the items on the flashcards, or make sentences. For example if everyone has a food or drink picture you could say: I like bananas and milk. The children with the picture of milk or bananas change places with each other. Other sentence ideas for different topics are:

Next weekend I'll windsurf and play tennis, or
On my farm there are pigs and sheep, or
My mum's a doctor and my dad's a dentist, or
On Monday I am going to the bank and the supermarket.

Listening and reading variant

Play the game as described above but using short phrases written on cards. For example write "Hello, how are you?" on one card and "I'm fine, thanks" on another. Write, "Where do you live?" on one card and "I live in India" on another, and so on until everyone has a card. Use this idea with sentences that you cut in half too.

After a few rounds the children swap papers with each other and take a turn with a different sentence. However bear in mind not to play for more than ten minutes to keep the game fresh and fun.

Speaking variant

To convert this into a speaking game let players take turns to call out the pictures that must be swapped. Give this job to your more advanced students to keep them challenged.

To make the game harder, have the person in the middle make up his or her own sentences with two of the given picture words in it. Be careful that your students are up to this or the game could drag.

ALPHABET A & B

Category: Listening and speaking variants
Group size: 2 to 30
Level: Beginners to learn the alphabet
Materials: Letters of the alphabet
Age: 5 to 12
Pace: Calm

How to play

Divide the class into groups of 2 to 4 children. Give each group a pile of letters and spell out a word. The children take the relevant letters from the pile and form the word on their table. With younger children give them a fewer letters to work with.

With a small group make several teams and have players come up and make the word on the front desks, before running back to their seats when finished. With a large group you would be better keeping children at their seats and working calmly in pairs. If necessary, to keep control of the class, play this game with the children working individually. With a mixed ability class use the more knowledgeable children as floaters to go around checking up on the words that are being formed.

Language ideas

To start with give out letters such as all the consonants and the vowel A. Spell easy words such as PAT, CAT, and FAT. Round two can be all the consonants and the vowel I, for words such as FIT, BIT and PIT. It is OK if the children do not understand all the words they make. The important thing is that they recognise the sounds and letters of the alphabet.

With young children call out the sound of the letter in the context of the word rather than naming the letter. For example the letter P in the word PAT would be "pe" not "pee".

Materials

Type letters in a large font or ask the children to write their own letters, one letter per piece of paper.

Alphabet B - speaking variant

How to play

You, or a class member, spell a word out loud. The first team has 3 seconds to name the word you spelled. If the team has not named the word within the 3 seconds the rest of the class is free to call out the word to win a point for their team.

To get all the children saying the words, have a rule where the whole team must call out the word within the three second limit. The quickest children will name the word first but the rest of the team must be listening and ready to chime in with the word before the three seconds are up in order for the team to win its point. If three seconds is too short extend the time limit to suit your class level.

No materials are needed. Use words that are harder to spell for older or more advanced children.

Anagrams

Category: Reading, spelling and speaking
Group size: any class size plus large class variant
Level: Beginner to Advanced
Materials: Sets of letters
Age: 4 to adult
Pace: Calm to excitable variants

How to play

Cut up words into letters and place these in zip lock bags, one word per bag. Stick to simple words such as CAT and DOG for 6 year old children. In order to make the task of deciphering the word fairly easy either give out words which are in the same family of vocabulary, such as food words or professions, or give out a clue with every set of letters, which can be written on a sticker on the bag. Give the signal to start. Players race to find their word, which they call out.

When everyone has their word the quickest to finish can help anyone who would like help. Players then put their letters back in the bag. Play some music while the bags are passed around the class until you turn the music off. The game continues with each player having a fresh bag to work with.

A variation is to have children working together and to give each team a pile of letters containing twelve words. Have pictures or clues of the words on the board, otherwise this is far too difficult. On your signal each team works together to form all the words from the pile. The first team to finish wins. Alternatively allow every team to finish and congratulate all teams as they finish.

Small group variation 1

Here is a more excitable team version of this game. Divide your class into small teams of three children each. Have piles of letters for each word at the front of the class, a different word per team. The first member of each team runs up to the front, forms the word, calls it out to their team-mates and runs and touches the next team-mate. This child now runs to the front (meanwhile you have swapped the letters over with a new word), forms a new word, calls it out to the team, runs back and touches the third team-mate who now has a turn. In order to keep your materials together you may disqualify any team that does not treat your letters carefully and put them ALL back into the bags!

Small group variation 2

Another fun way to play if you have a small group is to give each player or team a buzzer. The bells you often find on hotel receptions work well. Kids love the novelty factor of a bell and it is very easy to prevent them from ringing it all the time as you just deduct a point every time someone rings the bell without an answer. That works instantly!

Lay out or write up the scrambled letters of a word. All players try to figure out the word (give them a clue if necessary), and as soon as a player has the word he or she hits the buzzer to get a point for the team if correct.

Give the team a certain amount of time (10 to 15 seconds) to figure out a word, after which it is open to the buzzers of all teams. Rig the game to keep the teams close together by giving easier words to a team that is lagging behind, which they are more likely to guess in the timeframe, before the other buzzers can come in and steal the point.

Advanced variant

Give out the letters for sentences for advanced players. Here you would need to give a clue. Have a go at this game yourselves and you'll see that it can be difficult, so pictures or clues are necessary.

Another variant for all class sizes

Write up 12 words from a theme on the board and ask each pupil to pick a word and make an anagram of it. When everyone has written an anagram they swap it over with a neighbour. Clear the board and give a time limit for students to decipher the anagram and write the word out correctly.

The game is now to unite all the identical words together. Use the first part of the Kidnap game to do this. It is explained here for convenience: Let's say you are using furniture vocabulary with "here is / here are". One person with each piece of furniture stands up, so you have 12 children standing. The child with the table must collect in all the other tables.

The other children stay seated and make a mental note of the furniture on their paper, which they fold up into four, so the word cannot be read. All students pass their paper from hand to hand, telling the child they pass it to what it is, so that it may continue its way to the collector. This allows for such frequent repetition of these twelve words that your students will have them memorised by the end of the game.

Use simple target structures with this idea not just single vocabulary words. Keep the sentences short so that the papers can be passed quickly. Insisting on whispering will keep the overall noise level down.

Materials

Use plastic zip lock bags (like freezer or sandwich bags) to hold the letters of each word. For a full class you might want to give out 12 different words, repeated once if you have a class of 24 and repeated twice with a class of 36. For a quick way to prepare, print these words off, to be sure they are legible and save the document for future use with another class.

Backwards Bull's Eye

Category: Speaking - making sentences
Group size: 2 to 30
Level: Beginner to Intermediate
Materials: None or pictures
Age: 4 to 12
Pace: Calm to wake up

Put the children into teams. Draw a large target on the board such as a dartboard or a big circle. Write two known vocabulary words on the board. With the first word demonstrate how the game will be played. The students all think of a sentence containing that word. For a grammar drill this sentence can follow a specific structure or tense. For fluency and quick thinking let pupils make up any sentence containing the word.

All students have a few seconds to think something up, as no one knows who will be chosen. The teacher picks someone who says his or her sentence. If the student does not have a sentence ready, too bad, move straight on to someone else. There should be no waiting on an individual and this is important as it shows the class members that they must actively prepare a sentence EVERY time, regardless of whether picked to aim at the bull's eye or not.

The class decide if the given sentence is correct, with the help of the teacher if needed. If correct that student has a chance to aim at the bull's-eye and win a point for the team. To aim children stand with their backs to the board, bend down and aim at the board by looking between their legs. If this is not culturally acceptable for you then modify to suit your needs. For example children may aim by tossing the beanbag over their shoulder without looking at the board, or try to hit the target with eyes closed.

As soon as a child earns a chance to aim at the board the teacher writes up the next word so students can be mentally preparing their sentences. Give a ten second time limit for the creation of sentences, or a little longer if necessary, but be sure to keep this moving along so students spend most of their time thinking about sentences rather than sitting about while someone tries to throw something at the bull's-eye.

Consider putting children into pairs to work together at coming up with sentences. In pairs both children have a go at the bull's-eye simultaneously. This method is best for smaller groups where the noise level will be contained. Otherwise this game can be played in silence aside from students saying their sentences when chosen.

Balloon Fortunes

Category: Reading and speaking - good end of term game
Group size: 4 to 30
Level: Beginner to Intermediate
Materials: One balloon per child
Age: 6 to 12
Pace: Wake up

This is time consuming to prepare and is a nice idea for an end of term lesson or party rather than a regular lesson. Prepare some funny fortunes for your class members such as: You will marry a Martian and have 25 children. You will become a pop star. You will become an astronaut. For each fortune create a match such as: You become a Martian, marry a human and have 25 children. You will marry a pop star. You will build a space ship and become best friends with an astronaut.

You could ask your class to come up with funny fortunes for homework. Collect these in, correct them and use the students' ideas for the balloon fortunes game. The children's ideas of what is funny will probably work better than your own! Write out the fortunes on pieces of paper and place each paper inside a balloon, one balloon per child. These balloons all need blowing up and tying so good luck if you have a large class!

Start your end of term lesson with a bang by distributing the balloons and let the children each burst one and read the fortune inside. Students then have the task of finding their pair or matching fortune, i.e. the astronaut will pair up with the student who will build a space ship and become best friends with an astronaut.

With intermediate students or for more reading practice put a longer descriptive passage inside each balloon which students read and find their match. A description of how to build a space ship could match up with a description of how to become an astronaut. Again let the children write these for homework and correct the mistakes before inserting into the balloons.

To get more mileage out of the balloons before bursting them you could also play Don't Drop the Bomb or any of the passing games such as Hot Potato, Pass the Box or Pass the Pictures. Here use a balloon instead of a flashcard and when the music stops the child with the balloon bursts it and reads out the fortune.

Balls and Tenses

Category: Speaking
Group size: Small group.
Level: Beginner to Intermediate
Materials: One ball per group.
Age: 4 to Adult. Basic bouncing only for the 4 and 5 year olds.
Pace: Wake up

This game was given to me by a teacher called Ramey who uses it with his small groups of up to six students. He feels it would work in a classroom but I have my doubts, knowing how mental some boys go when they catch sight of a ball! However it is certainly ideal with small groups.

One student in the group bounces the ball in a given way that represents a certain tense. The other students then make up a sentence in that tense. Students take it in turns with the ball. With beginners use two tenses only. With intermediates mix up as many tenses as you need to in order for the game to be challenging, but not too hard.

Here are Ramey's ball movements and you'll notice that the left side represents the past while the right represents the present:

Simple present: bounce the ball straight down between your feet while alternating left and right hands. Younger children need not alternate hands.

Simple past: Hold the ball in your left hand with your left arm stretched out. Bounce the ball ONCE on the verb: e.g. We WENT shopping last week. Students take it in turns to make a sentence and bounce the ball on their verb.

Present Continuous/progressive: Walk in a circle to the right while bouncing the ball continuously.

Past Continuous/progressive: As for present continuous but walking to the left.

Present Perfect: Hold the ball in the right hand and bounce it diagonally between the feet, catching it with the left hand, then back the other way: e.g. They HAVE (right hand bounces to the left hand) DONE (left hand bounces to the right hand) their homework.

Past Perfect: Hold the ball in the left hand and bounce on HAD, step to the left and bounce again on the participle: e.g. They HAD (left hand bounce, one step to the left) EATEN (left hand bounce once) before they LEFT (left hand single bounce for Simple Past) for work.

Ramey and his students have a hilarious time with it, especially when they combine tenses (which means combining the bounces).

Bang

Category: Speaking

Group size: 2 to 20 for best results but can be played with more

Level: Beginner to Intermediate

Materials: None

Age: 4 to Adult

Pace: Wake up

This idea comes from a Vietnamese playground game and it can be used for basic vocabulary review, for drilling specific language or for fluency. Students form a circle with the teacher in the middle as the cowboy. The teacher pretends to shoot a student in the circle and fires a word or sentence at them. This student ducks and the children on either side must shoot each other with the answer. The fastest student who uses correct English wins and the other person is out. Continue until you have two students left. These two walk away from each other for four steps as the teacher counts up to four. Then the teacher calls out the word and the two students turn round and shoot at each other with the answer.

This works for small groups. If you have more than 10 students I recommend keeping players in the game rather than making them be out. Otherwise you'll have too many people hanging around on the sidelines, probably getting up to no good or chatting. Instead of players being out, each child has three lives. Play until one child loses all three lives and is out. At that point the game is over.

Here are some examples of how to drill language with this game:

Vocabulary ideas

For 4 and 5 year olds and for beginners play this with basic vocabulary where you say "green" and the other students say any other colour. If you say an animal they say any other animal. Bear in mind that with very young beginners they will have limited vocabulary and will not generally be that quick mentally at thinking things up out of the blue so stick to themes and words they know well, plus use picture prompts.

Another vocabulary variant is for you to say a word such as "cup" and the two students race to come up with any other word that starts with a C. Or use word association so if you say "cup" the students may say "tea" or "plate" and so on. Another idea is to play with parts of speech so you say a noun, they say a noun, you say a verb, they say a verb and so on.

Phrases

To drill short phrases the teacher says part of a sentence and the students add to it along specific guidelines. For example to practise adjectives the teacher may say: a girl. The students think an adjective to add to that and come back with: a pretty girl, a tall girl and so on. Do the same with adverbs. The teacher says: Read a book. The students say: Read a book slowly or read a book intelligently. Be sure to brainstorm adverbs beforehand.

Full sentences

For drilling specific grammar the teacher may say a word or phrase such as "Every morning". The students then make a sentence using the target structure and the vocabulary word. If the target structure is the present simple students could make a sentence such as "Every morning I brush my teeth". Phrases such as: every morning, every day, every evening and on Mondays are easy prompts for inventing a present simple tense.

Make it harder for more advanced students by giving a harder start. For example for sentences using "have you ever" the teacher can say: "blue eyes". Students invent a sentence such as "Have you ever seen a girl with blue eyes?"

If your students are struggling then make your prompts easier and simplify. Switch to phrases rather than sentences. The game must be quick to be fun rather than having students standing around scratching their heads. The idea is to get them talking.

Bangle or Bracelet Game

Category: Writing/Spelling

Group size: From six children up to any class size

Level: Beginner to Intermediate

Materials: One bracelet per team. Curtain rings are an alternative.

Age: 4 to 12

Pace: Wake up

How to play

This is a game made up by a teacher to wind up an English camp. It would be good at the end of a long day or to wake your pupils if they are tired. The pace of the game is lively though in theory it can be played in silence so there is no trouble with disturbing neighbouring classrooms here.

This is a variant of Relay Race but using bracelets (UK) or bangles (US). Any circular items will work such as curtain rings, copper or rubber plumbing seals, elastic hair ties or even elastic bands at a push though it will be faster with bracelets or similar.

Children stand in rows of three to eight per team with a pen in one hand. There should be a board or a piece of paper about 10 feet in front of them.

The last child in each row has a bracelet hung on the pen. When the signal to start is given, the last child passes the bracelet to the pen in front. This child takes the bracelet and passes it to the next child in line using only the pens. Children continue passing until the bracelet reaches the first child who runs to the board, writes the letter W, joins the line at the back and passes the bracelet to the child in front. Anyone dropping a bracelet has to start from the beginning at the back.

Each child writes a letter to have the sentence WE HAVE WON on the board. The first team to finish wins the game. Alternatively give the class various words to spell by saying the word to them as the signal to start. The winners are those who have spelled the most words correctly.

Bingo

Category: Listening
Group size: Any
Level: Beginner to Intermediate
Materials: None obligatory or one bingo set per player
Age: 4 to 12
Pace: Calm

How to play

Bingo is a game where the pupils each have a card with several numbers. The teacher calls out numbers randomly and when a number is called the pupil has on the card he or she circles it. When a pupil has circled all the numbers he or she says "Bingo!" and has finished.

Bingo is easy with a large class, even with 120 pupils. Your pupils make their own bingo grid by drawing or writing out 6 words of their choosing from a selection of 20 on the board. Allow a couple of minutes to create the grids; it should not use up much class time. Randomly call out the words on the board while the students circle them as they are called. When a student has circled all six words he or she has finished and stands up. Play until everyone has finished with the young ones and until you have several winners for older children.

Number bingo ideas

With any sized class and with no material have each class member write down four numbers between 1 and 10. Play Bingo as described above until the whole class has finished and is standing. This would practise numbers 1 to 10. Use this same version of the game for any sequence of numbers, such as 10, 20, 30, 40 etc. or 100, 200, 300, etc.

Language ideas

Bingo is a good game to use at the early stage of presenting language as it exposes players to frequent repetition of new vocabulary or grammar. With beginners limit yourself to naming the items "car, dress, pool and mansion", or be more detailed and specify "red dress, purple dress and green car". Expose your players to more vocabulary still by being more descriptive, "beautiful red dress, green sports car", or teach grammatical structures such as "I wish I had a green car". Using sentences encourages attentive listening and drills the grammar in the sentence.

Have a system in place to ensure you call each picture once. Put small flashcards into a bag or hat, naming each one as you pull it out, or use a list. Let your best student pull the items from the hat and name them.

Blind Painter

Category: Listening, speaking
Group size: 2 to a class in small groups
Level: Beginner to Intermediate
Materials: Pen and paper for a small group, the board for a class
Age: 4 to 12
Pace: Wake up

How to play

Each painter is blindfolded and must draw something like a face, a house, a person sitting on a chair, or an animal, etc. The painter gives a running commentary of the drawing, for example, "Here is the head, here are the arms, here are the hands and here is the left leg."

Younger children will find the result very funny while the older children like the novelty of the game but will tire of it sooner. The other players or team members chip in and help if the painter cannot remember the words.

If playing with a small group, each player can take it in turns to be the blind painter. However the minute you have bigger groups you want to have several blind painters at once so that people do not wait a long time for their turn. In a classroom situation have several blind painters at the board, and pin up large pieces of paper on the walls for more teams if necessary. In this case post your best students as group leaders to help with language.

Board Bash

Category: Listening, speaking
Group size: 2 to 30
Level: Beginner to Intermediate
Materials: Class board, optional pictures, bean bags
Age: 4 to 12
Pace: Wake up

Take in some beanbags. Split the class into two teams. For body parts draw a large body or face on the board. Call out a body part or a sentence such as "my leg hurts" and the student with the beanbag tries to hit the leg on the board with the beanbag. Award points for correct hits.

For other vocabulary stick picture cards on the board and either call out words or use sentences with the words in. Students listen for the word and throw the beanbag at the correct picture. A way to ensure all students listen carefully is not to designate the student who will throw the bag until after you have named the word or read out the sentence. If a student was not listening deduct a point from that team for negligence. This makes all students play all the time and not just the one with a beanbag.

It is important to keep the pace up otherwise imagine the time lag between goes with 20 students. Bring in different coloured beanbags, one colour per team, so two or three students aim at the board simultaneously. This will help give everyone a turn and keep the students interested. Students who have had a turn pick up the beanbags and give them out. Delegate score keeping and watching for hits. Students watching for hits stand at the side, then slap their hand in the place the beanbag struck and keep it there until the teacher evaluates whether it is accurate enough. The more people are actively participating in some way the less the class will mess around.

For a speaking variant ask the class questions. Students earn the chance to aim at the board through correct answers.

Bogeyman

Category: Listening, speaking
Group size: 2 to 30
Level: Beginner to Lower Intermediate
Materials: None
Age: 4 to 12
Pace: Excitable

Children love this game and it's a great excuse for repeating short dialogues.

How to play

This game is for small groups in a language school environment rather than a big class situation. Players pair up and have a set mini conversation with each other, such as:

Child 1: Hello
Child 2: Hello
Child 1: How are you?
Child 2: Fine thanks, and you?

As soon as child 2 says "and you?" he or she tries to touch child 1, metaphorically giving the other player the bogey, (if this is culturally acceptable for you of course). Give players a few seconds to transfer the 'bogey', then blow a whistle or give the signal for a new round to start. Players can swap partners after a few rounds. Use any mini-conversations for this game.

Ways to play with a larger class or to keep better control

Only allow the 'bogeyman' one go at touching the other player, and have a rule where children can only take one step. Depending on how your class is configured, you could also play this in pairs with your pupils seated, if they are not too close. It is possible to play this seated on the floor in pairs - close but not too close, so children still have to stretch to touch one another. This way the children cannot hurt themselves on any furniture in their excitement to pass on the bogey.

"Boggle"

Category: Spelling

Group size: 2 players to a large class divided into small groups or working individually

Level: Lower Intermediate to Advanced

Materials: The excellent game Boggle may be purchased in toy stores. One may also use the idea with letter flashcards or the board.

Age: From age 6. Use short words for ages 6 to 7

Pace: Calm

How to play – small groups

Place 9 letters in a zip lock back. Repeat with four more bags using different letters inside. Give each bag a different number.

Children work individually or in groups of 2 to 3. Hand out one set of letters per person or group and allow two minutes for the players to write down as many words as they can find in the given letters. When you say, "Stop" everyone puts the letters back in the bag and passes it on to the next person or group, receiving in turn a fresh bag from someone else.

The groups swap over their answer papers. Each group gives you its words and everyone gets 1 point for a valid word and 2 points for a word no one else has. If this points system is too complicated give one point per word regardless.

How to play – bigger groups to large classes

Playing with the bags and letters adds a dimension to the game and appeals to kinaesthetic and tactile learners because it's nice to touch the letters and move them around. It is not practical, however, to handle all those fiddly materials with a big class. Instead write a grid of letters on the board. Boggle has a grid of nine, three by three, but put up more letters for beginners to make it easier. Here is an example of a grid with 20 letters containing animal words. Animal words are dog, cat, lion, goat, bat, snake, bird, crocodile, tiger, rat, chicken, horse, hen, cockerel, kitten and maybe some more you will find! Tell the children to think of the animals they know in English, and then look and see if the letters are there. Display picture prompts to help.

L	O	A	D
I	C	C	L
O	G	E	S
N	R	T	K
B	T	H	B

Brainstorm

Category: Listening, speaking
Group size: 2 players to a class
Level: Lower Intermediate to Advanced
Materials: None
Age: 6 to adult
Pace: Wake up

How to play

Give each team twenty seconds to come up with as many words as possible in a given category and call them out as until the time is up. The other team or teams (and you) count the words. To prevent one student from taking over the whole game have a quota of one word per team member. Suggest to the better students that the team might earn more points if they let their team-mates go first. This means the better students have to think up less obvious words as the easy ones will be the first to be called out.

Once the twenty seconds are up the other teams have a chance to earn bonus points if they can name additional vocabulary in the category in the ten seconds following. You then give the next team a new theme for a twenty-second brainstorm. By all means lengthen the time limits if more appropriate to the level of your class, but always err on the side of giving too little time to keep up the element of adrenalin and fun. Categories can include cartoon characters, types of transport, musical instruments, animals, types of food, toys, jobs, countries, favourite characters, etc.

Use pictures, prompts and mimes to help elicit vocabulary as a way to help teams that are lagging behind.

Large class variant

Divide the class into teams and call out a theme. Each team calls out one word from that theme. The person who calls out the word stands up and cannot participate again in that round. Continue round the teams until everyone has run out of words. A team has five seconds to name a word. If the team cannot give a new word in that time limit move on to the next team to avoid delays that make the game drag. You may want to recruit a class member to be on a stopwatch for you.

When you start round two with a different theme, have another team start off, and go round the teams in the same order as before. The winning team, if you want to have a winner, is the one that contributes the most words.

Optionally have a member from each team at the board writing words his or her team contributes as the game is played. This allows you to easily count the words for each team at the end and be sure the same words are not used twice. It also reinforces the vocabulary further seeing it written on the board as well as hearing it spoken. Therefore if you have some pupils who are rather quiet during this game, fear not, at least they will be hearing and seeing the words, which is still helpful. Don't slow the pace of the game down for the writing, put more students at the board instead.

British Bulldog

Category: Speaking
Group size: 5 to 30

Level: Beginner to Intermediate
Materials: None. Optional picture cards
Age: 4 to 12
Pace: Excitable

Here is a version of the classic playground game which needs open space.

How to play

A player, the bulldog, stands in the middle with all the other players at one end of the room or playground. The players chant "Hello Mr. Bulldog, how do you do, who do you want to help you?" The bulldog replies, "I want ..." and names a child. This child runs to the other end of the room without getting caught by the bulldog. If the child is caught he or she stays in the middle and helps the bulldog catch the other players.

The bulldog can say "British Bulldog" at any moment, when all the players have to run to the other side. Those caught stay in the middle.

Language ideas

All sorts of language may be used with this game. Here is an example of a rhyme but do make up your own:

Players: Nice Mr. Bulldog, one two three
Nice Mr. Bulldog, don't pick me!
Bulldog: I pick Jacky!

Try this scenario. The room is a crocodile infested swampland. One player starts as a crocodile and all the others are gazelles, which have to cross the swamp without being eaten. As the crocodile catches the gazelles they become crocodiles. The gazelles are gathered on one side of the swamp and the crocodile says:

I'm hungry for my breakfast
I'm hungry for my brunch

I'm hungry for my dinner
And now I want my lunch!

The gazelles reply:
I know you want your breakfast
I know you want your brunch
I know you want your dinner
But I won't be your lunch!

All the gazelles then run across the swamp, dodging the crocodiles if they can. If a crocodile touches them they stay in the swamp and help catch the rest of the gazelles. The last gazelle to be caught is the crocodile in the next round.

Play with questions

Instead of using the same rhyme each time have players ask the bulldog any question, such as "What do you do?" or "Where do you live?" or "Where did you go this weekend?" etc. The bulldog replies and finishes each reply with someone's name. If asking the same question over and over request that the bulldog gives a different reply each time, such as "I went to the beach, I went to the cinema", etc. Show picture prompts if inspiration dries up.

Play with flashcards

Another version is to give each player a picture or word flash card, big enough for the bulldog to see. The players say their refrain or ask their question, such as: "Mr. Bulldog, what will you have for your tea?" The bulldog replies, "I'll have chips". The player with the chips has to run to the other side. A basic version would be for the bulldog to simply name the flashcards with no question and answer format.

With a big class the bulldog should request three things for his tea so more people have to run across. For example I'll have chips, egg and milk. This prevents the game from dragging.

Bucket Game

Category: Writing and thinking about grammar
Group size: Any class size
Level: Beginner to Intermediate
Materials: One container per team. Use the board or give out worksheets.
Age: 4 to 12
Pace: Calm

Not everyone gets to speak in this game, but everyone writes, listens and thinks about the target structure, and some people have a chance to read the answers out loud. Divide the class into teams. Have one bucket (or plastic bag) per team, labelled with the team letter or number.

Give your class an exercise such as a fill in the blanks, an anagram, a sentence to unscramble, or writing a question for an answer or an answer for a question. Each team leader takes the bucket around his or her team to collect the answers. With the buckets at the front, team leaders each pull out one answer, and read it out to the class. The class vote as to whether it is correct or not. If it is correct, that team wins a point, if incorrect, they do not score. Move on to the next team, and so on.

Repeat the whole thing for round two, but use different children to read out the answers if possible, and so on for about 15 minutes.

GAMES C-D

Call My Bluff

Category: Easy speaking

Group size: Divide the class into small groups of four to five children

Level: Beginners

Materials: Deck of picture or word cards for each group

Age: 4 to 12

Pace: Calm

This speaking game is based on a card game. Instead of using playing cards use decks of homemade cards showing vocabulary. These could be pictures or words. Word cards are quick to make and help with spelling. Picture cards help with vocabulary acquisition and retention.

It's important that the cards are not see-through so if using paper then write the words in pencil, or use light grey printer ink so the type does not show through and give the game away.

How to play

Let's say you would like to work on the days of the week. Make a sufficient supply of small cards, one day of the week per card. Students are dealt all the cards. The first person lays down any day of the week, face down and names the day, for example Tuesday. The next person HAS to lay down either the day before or the day after. If he/she does not have the correct day he/she has to bluff. If a player thinks the person is bluffing he/she challenges them. "You're bluffing!" If the person is bluffing he/she must pick up all the cards in the pile and add them to his/her hand. If he/she was telling the truth, then the challenger has to take all the cards.

Players can lay down more than one card at a time but they are inferring that they are all the same card, three Mondays for example. The winner is the one who has no cards left. Alternatively play for a set time limit then pupils count up their cards and the winner is the one who has the least cards.

To enhance speaking opportunities instruct pupils to use the target vocabulary in sentences each time they lay down a card. For example using days of the week and the present tense: I go skating on Mondays, I go sailing on Tuesdays, I play tennis on Wednesdays and so on.

Days of the week and months of the year follow an order but general vocabulary does not. An option therefore is to list words on the board and number them. For example:

1. Swimsuit
2. T-shirt
3. Shirt
4. Socks
5. Shoes

If a pupil plays a shirt the next player must play (or bluff) a T-shirt or socks.

Call My Bluff Grammar Variant

Category: Speaking

Group size: Divide the class into small groups of four to five children

Level: Beginners to Intermediates

Materials: Packs of playing cards

Age: 4 to 12

Pace: Calm

Play as for Call My Bluff. Assign a part of speech to each number word or picture. For example nouns, verbs, prepositions, Adverbs and conjunctions. Write those on the board as a reference. With younger children limit the parts of speech to verbs and nouns to start with.

Players must get rid of their cards by laying at least two of a kind down on the pile while describing what cards they are putting down, e.g. "Two conjunctions". To increase the speaking opportunity players can also be requested to name two conjunctions as well. To go a step further players make a sentence containing two conjunctions although this option is likely to make the game laborious for everyone other than advanced students. Make sure that the level of difficulty is within the capabilities of your students or the game will rapidly become extremely dull. As with Call My Bluff if a player does not have two of the same part of speech he or she has to bluff and hope the others do not catch him/her out.

Chanting Game

Category: Very easy speaking
Group size: 2 to 15
Level: Beginners
Materials: None, blindfold optional
Age: 4 to 12
Pace: Wake up

Thanks go to Linda Yechiel for giving me this game. It is an excellent game for learning vocabulary and gaining confidence speaking.

Variant needing blindfold and space

Blindfold one child and place a picture card or item somewhere in the room. The others guide the blindfolded child to the picture by chanting the word over and over again. Quiet chanting means the child is far away from the picture, louder chanting means the child is approaching the picture. Once the child has found the picture swap over and let a few more children have a go, but not necessarily every child. Keep it fresh and move onto something else quickly.

Variant with no blindfold for regular classroom

A variation of this game is to hide two pictures or items around the room and divide your group into two teams. One child from each team must find a picture with the group guiding him or her in the same way as above. No blindfold is needed in this version as the picture is hidden. The two teams race to have their seekers find their picture first. If two teams cannot play simultaneously time each team in turn.

Charades

Category: Speaking
Group size: 2 to 20
Level: Intermediate to Advanced
Materials: None
Age: 8 to adult
Pace: Wake up

How to play

This game is for higher levels only because it needs significant vocabulary. One person mimes a book, song or film title by acting out each word or miming the idea expressed in the whole title. Those watching have to guess the book, song or film. The player miming is not allowed to speak at all and starts by indicating if it's a book (pretend to hold an open book), a song (pretend to sing), or a film (pretend to hold a movie camera). The other players respond to the mime by calling out the answer, for example, "It's a film" or/and "It's a book". The player miming then specifies how many words are in the title, and the other players respond, for example, "5 words".

The player miming can then either act out the whole title or choose to act out one of the words, for example he or she might hold up 5 fingers and the audience responds with "fifth word". The actor mimes working in a factory until someone guesses "factory" correctly.

The student miming might then hold up 2 fingers to correspond to the "second word", and indicate that this is "a little word" by holding their thumb and forefinger close together, as if they were holding a small object between them. The audience responds with "a, the, it, an" etc. until someone says "and", which is the correct word in this mime. So far we have "and" and "factory". In this case the book and film is Charlie and the Chocolate Factory. With 8 and 9 year olds you might want to think up some good titles for them in advance that are easy to mime in case the children cannot think of any on the spur of the moment.

Players can also mime syllables of words. For example hold up two fingers for second word, and then place one finger on your forearm to indicate first syllable. Mime making a pot on a wheel to get the first syllable "pot" of the word Potter for a Harry Potter film. In addition to syllables one can also mime things that sound like the word. The person miming holds a hand up to his or her hear and the players respond with 'sounds like'. One might mime "carry" with "sounds like" "Harry" to get "Harry Potter". It's best to play with the basics first and add in these refinements once the children are used to the game.

Charades Race

Category: Speaking
Group size: 2 to 30
Level: Beginner to Advanced
Materials: None
Age: 4 to adult
Pace: Wake up

How to play

Copy a chart onto the board with vocabulary categories you wish to review. Allocate points for each category, the higher the points the harder the word.

Emotions	Happy 100 points	Sad 200 points	Angry 300 points	Satisfied 400 points

For each category, write out a teacher's sheet with the nouns or words and the points they are worth. For example:

Categories	Point Score			
	100	200	300	400
Animals				
Feelings				
Food				
Jobs				

Score Board	
Team A	Team B

Divide the class into two teams and invite one or two students to come up and select a category and a number of points, such as animals for 200 points, or jobs for 400 points. Show the animal, feeling or job to be acted out for those points to the student at the front only. This student acts this out to their fellow team members. Give a one-minute time limit for the team to correctly guess the answer. If successful the team is awarded the points. If Team 1 are unsuccessful, Team 2 has a chance to guess and win the points instead.

As a variation have two students from each team acting up front, as a ruse to involve more people actively, either both acting the same word or a different one and the first team to guess correctly wins the point.

A student fills in the answers on the board as the game progresses. At the end the team with the highest points wins.

Grammar review

Aside from reviewing vocabulary use this game for sentences or grammar. For example the different squares can contain verb tenses such as present tense, present continuous, past continuous and past simple, the past simple being worth the greatest number of points. Students make up a sentence using the correct tense to win the point. Expand this idea for any grammar, any types of sentence or question. For example for questions fill in the chart with: where, why, how, what, which, do, does. Students pick their square and make a question starting with that question word.

What	Where	Do	Does	Which	How	Why
100	200	300	300	400	400	500

Pronunciation

Use the game also for phonemes or pronunciation. If you have a single nationality class all students are likely to have trouble with the same sounds and these can be worth the highest points.

Chinese Whispers

Category: Speaking (vocabulary, grammar, phonemes)
Group size: Any
Level: Beginner to Intermediate
Materials: None
Age: 4 to 12
Pace: Calm

How to play

I believe this game is called Chinese Whispers in England because it is hard to understand whispering, as it is hard to understand Chinese if you don't speak it. No offence is meant towards the Chinese with the name of this game. One player starts off whispering something to the person next to them who whispers it in turn to the person next to them and so on round the group. The last person then says the phrase or sentence out loud. Usually it is not the same as the initial message, which children find funny, although for the purpose of learning English this is not the point.

In order to encourage proper listening and speaking offer a point to the team that does succeed in transmitting the message correctly, otherwise the children distort it deliberately as that is normally the funny part of the game. Either award a point to the fastest team with the CORRECT message, or award a point to all teams that have the correct message and in this case give out different messages to each team.

A good group size is around 8 players. With a class either divide children into teams or pass several messages around the class at intervals of five to six people to keep the players involved. With a large class let students pass the message down the rows of the classroom, or along benches from one side to the other.

While all the messages are travelling down do not interrupt the game to read out the results but have students write them down at the end of the line and announce them all at the end. Players can also write the correct messages on the board.

Language ideas

Send any message down the line from very simple sentences to long and complex ones. You could also send down silly rhymes such as:

One banana, two bananas, three bananas, four
Five bananas, six bananas, seven bananas, more
Or from Snow White:
Mirror, mirror on the wall, who is the fairest of them all?

For older children send tongue twisters or more challenging sentences round. See the rhymes, riddles and proverbs for ideas.

Colour the Card

Category: Speaking
Group size: Pair work for any class size
Level: Beginner to Intermediate
Materials: Pairs of pictures – one coloured and one black and white
Age: 4 to 12
Pace: Calm

How to play

Divide your group into pairs. Give player 1 a coloured picture and give the other player the same picture but in black and white. Player 1 must not show the coloured picture to player 2. Player 2 has to ask what colour the items are in the picture so that he or she can colour it in. For example a picture of a lady in a dress player 2 can ask questions like: "What colour is the dress, what colour are the shoes, what colour is her hair, what colour is her belt?" I noticed in my classes that boys preferred to colour knights and cars to girls in dresses but there was always a choice and it's best to allow players to choose a picture they like. Either that or offer something bland bearing in mind that bland can be dull. As player 1 replies "The dress is red, her shoes are white", etc. player 2 takes the relevant colour and puts a dash of it on the picture, but does not colour the whole thing in at this stage. Once player 2 has made a note of all the colours the players swap roles with a different picture. When player 1 has all the colours down either let children colour their pictures in all together or take them home and do it later if they feel like it. You certainly do not want to spend much precious class time colouring in with older children. You can always compromise and colour for a few minutes and then leave children to finish in their own time. Consider displaying pictures children have finished at home in class as recognition of the child's motivation.

Materials

One way to make these is to print a coloured clip art picture and then save the image in greyscale or black and white. If you do not know about clip art try taking coloured pictures from magazines or children's storybooks and taking a black and white photocopy.

A way round the problem of finding or creating pairs of pictures is to give out black and white pictures to both children. The children themselves then decide what colour the items in the picture will be.

Colour Wolf

Category: Listening or speaking (colours or articles of clothing)
Group size: Small group or large class variant
Level: Beginners
Materials: None
Age: 4 to 12
Pace: Excitable and calm version for large class

Small group variant

This is a fun version of 'Tag' or 'It'. The wolf calls out a colour. If you are wearing it you are safe. If you are not wearing it then the wolf can catch you. The wolf has 15 seconds to catch someone not wearing the specified colour. If the wolf catches someone they become the next wolf and can immediately call out the new colour. If a wolf cannot catch anyone after two or three goes, change over. Blow a whistle after the 15 seconds so players know when time is up.

In the listening version the teacher calls out the colour and one of the children is the wolf. In the speaking version the wolf calls out the colour directly. You could do a variant on this game with articles of clothing or with vocabulary pictures that children hold in a way the wolf can see them.

Large class variant

The wolf stands at the front, facing the board. Students stand at their desks or benches. The wolf calls out a colour. If a pupil is wearing it, he or she gets eaten and sits down. If children all wear the same colours or uniform, then each pupil draws a circle in a chosen colour on a piece of paper and holds that up to their chest.

Play this game with any vocabulary. Each pupil writes or draws an object from a selection and holds the picture up to their chest as above for the colours. Use any target structure. The wolf says a sentence or question that includes one of the items from the selected vocabulary. For example let's say you want to introduce the present continuous. Pupils mime a sport from a list of suggestions, or write one down and hold up the paper. The wolf mimes and says, "I am fishing". All those pupils who have chosen fishing are eaten and sit down.

The winners are those left standing at the end. One of them can be wolf in the next round, or you might end it there.

Commands Race

Category: Listening
Group size: Any
Level: Beginner to Intermediate
Materials: None
Age: 4 to 12
Pace: Wake up

How to play

Divide the class into teams. Children are seated at their desks. Give a command such as run, jump, hop, or skip. All children stand up, carry out the action and sit down as fast as possible. The team finishing last gets a forfeit. Potentially give forfeits for pathetic mimes or messing about. See Copycat Commands just below for a list of ideas for actions.

Copycat Commands

Category: Listening
Group size: Any
Level: Beginner to Intermediate
Materials: None
Age: 4 to 12
Pace: Wake up

How to play

This is a simple game where you tell the class to do certain actions while miming them and they copy you. It is good for the initial introduction of vocabulary and also for quick revision of vocabulary before a game such as Simon Says. As your class become familiar with the language stop miming and just give the commands.

Here are some examples, assuming you are in a classroom and not in a playground, where there are more active possibilities. Add freely to them:

Dance / Jump / Run on the spot / touch your nose / touch any body part / touch a colour / touch an item of clothing / touch a friend's leg, arm, etc. / open a book / pick up a pen / fold a piece of paper / pass the paper to a neighbour / screw up the paper / throw it at someone / pick it up / unfold it/ write you name on it / be silent / crouch down / mime a chicken / write the number 7 / sing do re mi / tap your feet / clap your hands once / clap your hands five times / stand up / sit down / stand up if you're wearing a skirt / sit down if you are wearing shoes / stand up if you like tennis / sit down if you like chocolate / be a Jedi knight / be a princess / be a prince / fly a plane / drive a car / eat a melon / eat a sticky toffee pudding / hop on one foot / make the letter T with your hands / make the letter D with another child / be happy / look up / look down / look around / look out of the window / look under your desk / etc.

Counting and Number Games

Add up the Dice – speaking, age 6 upwards

Roll three dice and have players add up the total. With a big class bring someone up to roll the dice and write the three numbers on the board or call them out. Use giant dice or divide your class into smaller groups.

To practise higher numbers say that each number on the dice is x10 or x100 its face value. So 6 would become 60 or 600. 6 could also become 66 and 5 become 55 and so on.

Large class variant

Divide your class into teams of up to 10 pupils, or one row or bench per team. Name one pupil as the starter and another as the finisher per team. Write an easy sum on the board such as 4+3x2. On the word "Go" the starter whispers the answer to his team-mate, who passes it on. Any team member may give the answer to the starter if he or she works it out faster, but players must pass the answer down the line to the starter, they cannot call it out. The answer must then go through every player from the starter to the finisher which means it may travel up and down the line more than once depending on where the starter and finisher are sitting.

Allow only whispering to control noise. To control content only the answer may be spoken. Use of any other word, or any talking incurs a penalty for the team, or a disqualification in that round.

Clap and Count – speaking, all ages

Clap or bang a number of times and have the class call out how many times you clapped. Put children into pairs and have them play with each other. With younger children clap slower so they can follow you, and with older ones make it quite difficult by clapping as fast as possible. Pupils may also play this in pairs.

Count the Cards – listening, all ages

Give out 10 to 20 cards per player. The players must count out the number you tell them as fast as possible. Say something along the lines of, "On your marks, get set, 3!" Players count out three cards and then put their hand up saying, "finished!" or "3!"

You won't want to make it a race for 4 to 5 year olds, but just have them count out the cards in their own time. If the same person keeps winning all the time have them call out the numbers.

To ensure no cards are mislaid - and this is a good tip for all the games - have your group leaders collect them and have everyone count their cards back into the bag or basket, or appropriate receptacle.

Guess the Price – speaking, all ages

Hold up an item. Each player writes down a price and the winner is the one who either guesses the price of the item or gets closest to it. An option to avoid cheating is to have players swap their paper with a neighbour. Ask any player for his or her price. Respond saying whether the actual price is higher or lower. If it is higher all those with lower prices know they have lost. Continue asking players for their prices until the winner is identified.

For beginners the prices can be simple such as 1 dollar or 3 dollars. For advanced players have things priced at 1 dollar 98 cents, or 358 dollars and 43 cents, etc. Use different currencies to teach dollars, euros, pounds, or yen, etc.

The class may be divided into groups with the best pupils as group leaders to hold up the card and ask for the prices.

How Many? – speaking, all ages

Place a number of items around the room at 'guessing stations' and have all the players circulate freely, visiting each station and guessing how many items there are. Use things such as:

A jar of coins

A jar of sweets

A bag of small objects
A transparent bag of biscuits
A transparent bag of peanuts
A pile of magazines
A pile of papers
A page full of words
A pack of envelopes

Give a fairly tight time limit to complete the task to keep everyone focused. Once all the players have written down their guesses make two teams either side of the room. Ask (or have a pupil ask) a question relating to "guessing station 1", for example: "How many coins are there in the jar?" A volunteer player from Team 1 answers, "There are 30" or, "I think there are 30 coins in the jar". Write 30 under Team 1.

Tell players whether the number is higher or lower. If the number is higher any player on Team 2 who has a higher number offers their guess, for example, "There are 55". Write 55 under Team 2. Tell players whether the number is higher or lower and those still in the running give their guess until you get as close as possible to the actual number of coins. Each time a closer guess is given write it up for the team and rub out the previous guess which is further away from the truth.

Now move on to the second 'guessing station'. Go through the process as described above. Continue to note the best guesses of each team until you have gone through all the guessing stations, and then write the actual number of items at each station, awarding a point to the closest team. If a team gets the number bang on you could give double points.

Match Stick Game – speaking, age 6 upwards

This is the classic game where players each have 3 matches or small items behind their backs. Sitting in a circle, each player takes between 0 and 3 matches and hides them in their fist. All players hold out their fist in the middle of the circle, the object being to guess the total number of matches in all the hands. Each player takes a guess. If someone says 6, no one else can say 6 in that round. Aside from numbers this game can also be used to practise "I think there are", "There are", "I believe there are".

Pass the Ball – speaking, all ages, small groups

To learn to count from 0 to 20, pass a ball round with every one counting in unison. When the players become good at counting have only the player throwing the ball say the number. 4-5 year olds can roll the ball across the floor. I have observed a tendency for some boys to go into a frenzy of excitement when they get near a ball and if that is the case for your pupils then replace the ball with another item that must be passed from hand to hand rather than thrown. With more than 15 children pass two or more balls round at once to avoid boredom.

To learn higher numbers count in tens: 10 20 30 40 50, or count up in 2s: 2 4 6 8 10 12, or in 3s: 3 6 9 12 15, or count all numbers with a 9 in them: 9 19 29 39 49 59 69 79 89 91 92 93 etc. Use this game for the alphabet too.

When the class become good at this, whistle or clap to signal a change in direction and count down instead.

Telephone Game – listening, all ages

Ask pupils to write a number between 0 and 10 on a piece of paper or give out laminated numbers if you have them. Divide the class into two teams. Call out a five-digit telephone number for Team 1. The pupils listen and if they are holding one of the numbers they hold it up. Team 2 check it is correct and point out any errors. Call out a different phone number for Team 2.

With a small group take it a step further, call out a five-digit number and ask pupils to stand in the correct order. Read out the number twice and use a time limit to keep pupils alert and the game moving on.

Fizz Buzz, Don't Drop The Bomb and Higher or Lower are also suitable for numbers.

Dancing Demons

Category: Speaking
Group size: 3 to 21
Level: Beginner
Materials: Picture or word flashcards
Age: 4 to 12
Pace: Wake up to excitable

How to play

This game only works with small groups as it takes time to attach pictures to people's backs. It could also become too chaotic with a full class. For small groups it is an excellent 5-minute game to practise vocabulary with plenty of movement.

In groups of three pin a picture on to the back of every player. Your class can do this to each other - although not with people in their own group of three, as the others in the group must not see the pictures. The group of three face each other and jump around trying to glimpse the picture on the backs of their two contestants, without allowing them to see the picture on their own back.

Ideas for organising the group

Once someone's picture has been identified that person waits in a given spot (backs to the wall so people will not see their pictures) until other people arrive whose picture has also been seen in round one, and then they can play a second round together.

Alternatively children form a circle and watch those in the middle. When someone's picture is named that child sits down and a child from the circle takes his or her place. In this variation allow one minute per round so there is a rapid changeover of children prancing about in the middle of the circle.

Decoding

Category: Listening and Spelling

Group size: Any
Level: Beginner to Intermediate
Materials: None or pictures
Age: 6 to adult
Pace: Calm

Display a code on the board where numbers are equal to letters. For example: 348 = a, 468= b, 708= c. The teacher reads out a number and students write down the corresponding letter until a word is formed.

For vocabulary use words instead of numbers. For example display the following on the board:

Pig = A
Chicken = I
Duck = L
Sheep = M
Cow = N
Frog = S

The teacher or a selected student reads out the words Pig, cow, chicken, sheep, pig, duck and frog. The class write down the corresponding letters and find that they have spelled the word 'animals'. In this task students benefit from seeing how words are spelled on the board while hearing how they are pronounced. To revise meanings rather than spellings place animal flashcards next to the letters instead of the written words.

Detective Game

Category: Speaking
Group size: Small group to a class of up to about 30
Level: Beginner to Intermediate
Materials: None
Age: 4 to 12
Pace: Calm

How to play

One child is chosen to be the detective and one child the thief. The detective has three chances to find the thief. To find the thief the detective chooses three children and asks each of them a question. The question can be any question form that you would like to practise such as "What is your name? Where do you live? What were you doing last night?" etc. The child answers the question accordingly and if the child is the thief he must give himself up for arrest after answering the question. If the detective has not found the thief after asking three children a question someone else takes over as the detective until the thief is found, or you could say that the thief got away and choose a new thief and a new detective for the next round.

The above set up works well for a small group of up to ten children. With more than ten pick more thieves and detectives to ask and answer questions simultaneously so that more children are involved in speaking.

Variation 1: An exciting variant is to allow the detective to ask as many children as possible in a given time frame. If you have some kind of audible timer it adds an element of pressure. Allow the detective two minutes to find the thief only and then play another round. If you divide the whole class into two teams, record which team finds the most thieves during the course of the game.

Variation 2: Another way to use the same idea but with a different scenario for variety is to reverse the procedure. Instead of the detective trying to find the thief you could have a situation where the child asking the question does not want to find the answer. For example have a wicked witch who turns you to stone if you speak to her. The questioner could play an imaginary character of your choosing and must ask three children a question. If one of those three children is the wicked witch then the questioner is turned to stone and has to be released by the whole class chanting a spell.

4 Games for Directions

Directions 1: Blind Directions

Category: Listening and speaking
Group size: 2 to 30 in pairs or fours and larger class variant
Level: Beginner to Intermediate
Materials: Blindfolds
Age: 4 to 12
Pace: Wake up

Small group variant with space

Everyone loves this game, even adults. Lay out a course to follow. Create this by placing books on the floor between the start line and the finish line. Put children in pairs or groups of four. Line up as many pairs as you have room for on the start line. You need one course per pair of children so you will probably only have room for two to three courses unless you play outside.

Blindfold player A of each pair on the starting line. Player B directs player A through the obstacle course to the end using directions such as: "Go straight on. Stop. Go left. Go right". Complicate the vocabulary used as the level of your class evolves. Four year olds may not know the difference between left and right in which case use go, stop and turn. The idea is for each pair to reach the finish line before the other pairs. A referee can accompany each pair to make sure that the directions are given in correctly if you like.

Large class variant with no space

If there is no space in your classroom or you have too many pupils adapt the game as follows: Decide on an obstacle course around the classroom - in between rows of desks, round the bin and back or whatever, and have only one blind folded person do the course while half the class (team A) whisper directions all together. Time this and then team B has a go directing their person, (you have to change the course a little once their player is blindfolded) and see which team gets through the course first. Two or three goes for each team of this will be enough.

Another way to adapt the game to the classroom is to make one long course through the class and have pairs set off close behind each other at intervals, with a referee checking the language. Have a rule where only whispering is allowed and anyone talking is out, or has to start from the beginning again.

Materials

For a blindfold airline eye pads work best, as you do not waste time tying them up the way you do with a scarf. There are children's masks in supermarkets at Halloween and if you tape over the eyeholes you'll have a blindfold.

Directions 2: Grandma's Directions

Category: Speaking - giving directions
Group size: any
Level: Beginner
Materials: None, space in aisles of class helpful
Age: 4 to 12
Pace: Wake up

This is a version of Grandmother's Footsteps. You, or a class member, are Grandma standing with your back to the class. Grandma calls out directions such as: "left, turn left, go left, right, go straight on, go backwards, go forwards and stop". You can add adverbs to these commands, such as "quickly".

At any moment Grandma suddenly turns round. Everyone must instantly freeze and anyone seen moving by Grandma goes back to the start. The idea is to creep forward when Grandma is not looking and touch her.

Directions 3: Directions on the Board

Category: Speaking - giving directions
Group size: any
Level: Beginner

Materials: Blindfold and large class variant with no materials
Age: 4 to 12
Pace: Wake up

Draw a grid on the board and write a number or letter in each square of the grid. Blindfold a child and tell him or her to circle a particular number or letter by following the directions given by the rest of the class. To add some fun divide the class into two or three teams and let each team guide their team member trying to beat the time of the other teams to accomplish the task.

Large class variant

Play this in pairs. One student sits with his head lowered into the crux of his left arm so he cannot see what his right hand is writing and the other student guides him to draw the circle around the number that you call out. Then swap the roles over.

Directions 4: Elastic Band Game

Category: Speaking - commands and directions
Group size: Small group activity because of fiddly preparation
Level: Beginner to Intermediate
Materials: Thick elastic bands and small objects
Age: 6 to 12
Pace: Calm

Thanks to teacher Jima for sending me this idea. This is a fun coordination game ideal for practising giving directions. Put the children into small groups of three or four and give out one or two objects and a thick elastic band per group. A potato would be a good object to use or any other unbreakable object.

Tie strings at equal intervals around a heavy-duty elastic band. You need one string per participant. Players work together to pick up and move objects to a specified location by pulling on the strings to open the elastic and lower it over the object they must move. Reverse the process to release the object once moved.

To use this idea for speaking practice ask the children to play with blindfolds except for one child who must tell the others what to do by giving commands and directions such as, pull on the strings, stop, lift, Jacky go left, Richard go right, etc.

Don't Drop the Bomb

Category: Speaking – counting, the alphabet or vocabulary
Group size: small group activity
Level: Beginner to Intermediate
Materials: None
Age: 4 to 12
Pace: Calm

Keep a balloon up in the air counting every time someone taps it. Pretend it is a bomb that will explode if it touches the floor. Make sure it never does actually explode with four year olds. For older children have a rule where players cannot touch the balloon twice in a row.

Use this idea to practise counting, saying the alphabet or saying any vocabulary, randomly or in themes.

Draw

Category: Listening
Group size: 2 to 40
Level: Beginner to Intermediate
Materials: Class board with pens
Age: 4 to 12
Pace: Wake up

This is a simple game where you call out an item and members of the class race up to the board to draw it. To organise this count round the class from 1 to 5 repeatedly and each pupil retains the number you give. Then call out an item and ask all the number 1s to come and draw it. To add a time limit the rest of the class count up to 20 and all the number 1s must complete their picture by the time the class have reached 20. If you like let the class pick out the best-drawn picture.

If you have 40 students or so bring up as many as possible at each round to keep waiting time down. For example if 5 students fit at the board then have 8 teams of 5. In this case you will have 8 rounds and everyone will have had a go. The more teams the better.

Dress Up

Category: Speaking
Group size: 4 to 30
Level: Beginner to Intermediate
Materials: Clothing and accessories such as belts, hats or scarves
Age: 4 to 12
Pace: Wake up

How to play

Divide your group into two teams. Team A will start by dressing up so allow a minute or two for this with one item per player minimum. Give Team B one minute to look at team A and memorise who is wearing what. Team B then turn away and cannot look at team A while team A has one minute to switch items of clothing or accessories. Team B then turn round and call out the changes that have taken place. Allow perhaps three minutes for this to give time to use the language. Give a point for each correct change noted, if you are scoring. Here are some examples of language:

Simplest: Point to the item that has changed ownership and say "the hat" or "black hat"

Or: Harder: Elisa is now wearing the black hat

Or: Possessives: Elisa is wearing John's hat

Or: Present and past continuous: Elisa is wearing the black hat and before she was wearing the pink skirt

With four and five year olds you want to make the task easier. Use fewer items and make fewer changes each time and make them obvious.

Materials

Optionally ask your class or group to bring fancy dress items with them that day. Fun items are long fluffy scarves made out of fake feathers, shawls, extravagant skirts and hats, cowboy hats, gun holsters, waistcoats, Mexican hats, etc. Save time by using a few different coloured hats and scarves as these are quick to put on. You might even use the children's own hats and scarves if it is cold but take care that the items are well-treated.

Dress up variant

The above game can be adapted to any vocabulary. Instead of dressing up give out picture cards of vocabulary. One team looks at the other and tries to memorise who has what. The team with the pictures do a swap amongst themselves and the other team spots the difference. The players practise saying things like "John had the car", "John had the car and now he has the bus", "John has Eli's bus".

Dress Up Race

Category: Listening
Group size: From 4 players to groups of a maximum of 8 each
Level: Beginner
Materials: Clothing and accessories
Age: 4 to 12
Pace: Wake up

Use this game when presenting new clothing vocabulary or to revise it. For each group you need a pile of clothing and / or accessories. For younger children you might want to have two of each item (not necessarily identical). Divide the group into pairs and tell the first pair the item they are to fish out of the pile and put on. Put on some trousers - Ready steady GO! Then pupils race to take the items off.

Duck, Duck, Goose

Category: Speaking
Group size: Small group to a large class
Level: Beginner
Materials: None
Age: 4 to 12
Pace: Wake up

How to play

Players sit in a circle. One player, who we will call A, walks quickly round the outside of the circle gently tapping the seated players on the shoulder saying "duck" each time. When A says "goose!" the child touched on "goose" gets up and chases A round the circle, trying to catch him or her before A runs a full circle and takes the place of the "goose". The "goose" never catches the one who touched him so everyone has a go. Each round change the vocabulary, for example, sticking to the animal theme have, "tiger, tiger, snake!" followed by, "cow, cow, pig!"

Using a rhyme or song

Use a rhyme instead, which the whole group says in unison. See the rhymes section for ideas. While the group chant the rhyme someone goes round the circle touching each child, until the group says the last word of the rhyme. At this point the person touched gets up and chases the one who touched him or her round the circle.

Large class variant

This game is a great excuse to say the same words over and over so that pupils memorise them and have plenty of opportunity to say them out loud.

Every tenth pupil screws up a piece of scrap paper into a ball. Using two of your chosen words the class say them rhythmically and steadily in unison, as follows, "duck, duck, goose; duck, duck, goose; duck, duck, goose" etc. Each time the third word is said the paper is passed along the line of students and through the class. Work out a simple route through the class that the paper balls must follow. Once the paper reaches the back of the class it can be passed back the same way or follow a circuit (easier).

Say "stop!" unexpectedly on the word "goose". All the children who are geese at that moment stand up and mime being geese or do a forfeit, all together to avoid waiting time. Continue using two different animals or other vocabulary words of your choosing.

GAMES E-G

Figure It Out

Category: Writing
Group size: 1 to 30
Level: Beginner to Advanced
Materials: Optional picture flashcards or objects
Age: 6 to 12
Pace: Calm to Wake up

If possible prepare sets of picture cards or objects to each represent a theme, if this is too much work then use words. For example:

School: Book, pencil, desk, chair, table, black board
Beach: Sea, sand, shells, towel, sunglasses, suntan lotion
Airport: Plane, runway, terminal, ticket, check-in
Restaurant: Waiter, tables, chairs, food, plates, kitchen, till
Cinderella: Glass slipper, pumpkin, a couple of ugly sisters, a princess, a prince

For the older children be a little more cryptic, for example:

Chocolate cake: chocolate, flour, butter, cake decoration, candles
Police station: policeman, handcuffs, key, parking ticket

Hairdressers: hairbrush, scissors, money, mirror

Disperse the sets of pictures or clues about the class give a 1-2 minute time limit at each clue for people to guess the theme these clues belong to. Students write down the answer. Your class can work individually on this one or in pairs or groups if the children stay on task when unsupervised. Every two minutes make sure everyone moves onto a different theme. Allow an additional 2 minutes to go through all the answers.

Materials

If you want to make the effort, put together real items in bags and place these around the class at 'stations'. The children circulate freely and have a time limit to work out all the clues. If you have children's toys at home you'll find these very useful. If you have no space and no materials use written clues that children work out at their desks.

Find the Pairs Memory Game A

Category: Speaking
Group size: 2 to a class divided into groups of up to 6
Level: Beginner to Intermediate
Materials: Two matching sets of pictures cards per group
Age: 4 to 12
Pace: Calm

How to play

Take two sets of identical pictures, shuffle them and spread them out face down. The pictures can be laid out randomly or in a grid. Player 1 turns over two cards and names the items. If they are a pair player 1 keeps the cards. If they are not a pair he or she turns them back over, leaving them face down in the same place. Player 2 now turns over two cards, attempting to turn over identical pictures, and names the items. The game continues until all the pairs have been found. The younger the players the fewer pairs you lay out initially.

In the classic game when a player turns over a pair he or she gets another go. However as the goal is to have the group master language rather than find a winner, it is preferable to let each person have only one turn. This makes it less likely for the brighter person to win all the pairs leaving the others with nothing.

A nice way to keep everyone interested, even when it is someone else's turn, aside from the fact that they are supposed to be memorising the cards, is to split each group into two teams. Each person has a go as normal, however the team-mates can help with vocabulary if need be. When counting up all the pairs at the end one can have a winning team rather than a winning individual.

Language ideas

The language possibilities with this game are numerous, keeping an eye as always on the complexity, so that the game does not drag.

Vocabulary: Each player names the items on the cards he or she turns over.

Phrases: Each player forms a short phrase including the item on the card. For example with pictures of people one could use adjectives such as "a pretty girl", "a tall boy", or with places "a big city", "a small village".

Sentences: Each player forms a sentence using one or both of the items. For example if you are using pictures of food players can say: "I like butter and milk", or "I like butter but I don't like milk". If you are using pictures of people players can say; "Her name is Claudia" or "She is a dentist", or "She is from Spain", or "She is wearing trousers", etc. One can also work on comparatives such as "the girl is taller than the boy", or "the girl is older than the baby". More advanced students can practise more complicated structures, depending on the language you would like them to learn. For example, "I was going to buy some milk but I bought some cheese instead", or "I have never been to London but I have been to Paris".

Questions: Players ask questions related to each picture they turn over. For example with sets of people ask, "What's her name?" "Where does she live?" or "How old is she?" For example Team 1 asks, "Where did you go last summer?" A player from Team 2 turns over two cards and replies, "I went to London and Paris".

Materials

Use pictures for best results when learning vocabulary. Word cards are fine if you are practising sentences. With children under the age of 6 it is recommended to use only pictures.

Find the Pairs Memory Game B

Category: Reading and speaking
Group size: 2 to a class divided into groups of up to 6
Level: Beginner to Intermediate
Materials: Two matching sets of word flash cards
Age: 6 to 12
Pace: Calm

To be played in the same way as Find the pairs memory game A, using word flash cards instead of pictures, to work on spelling and reading. Make up phrases, sentences and questions in exactly the same way with these words as with the pictures, as described above.

Find Your Friend

Category: Speaking
Group size: Small groups to a class of 40
Level: Beginner to Advanced
Materials: Small cards or pieces of paper
Age: 4 to 12
Pace: Wake up

How to play

Give out one card or picture with a place on it to each child. If you have thirty children you might give out 6 to 8 different cards. The children have to find out who else lives in the same place as they do. For example use pictures of major cities and countries. This is nice because it educates the children in a general way as well as teaching English. The children go around asking, "Where do you live?" The child who is asked replies, "I live in Paris", or "I live in France". If this is a match then the two pair up and continue looking for other children who live in the same place.

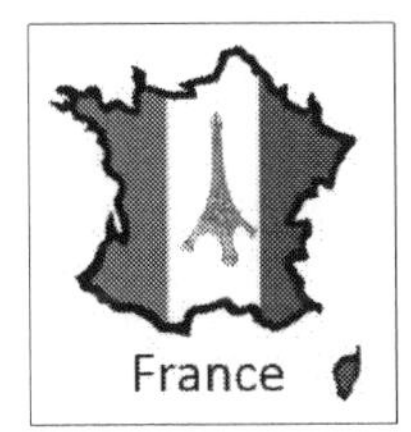

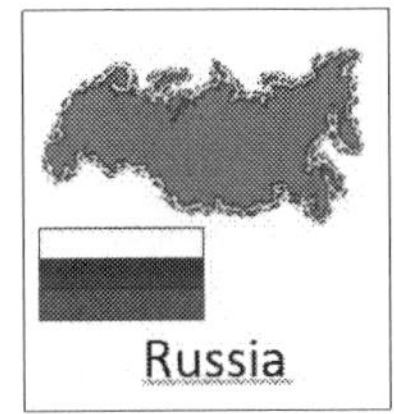

Think up pairs of words that go together, such as hair and hairbrush and have pictures of hair and a hairbrush, or two word flashcards with one word on each. Shuffle and hand out one card per player. Players keep their cards hidden and find their other half through dialogue.

With younger children give out identical pairs of pictures so they can match dog with dog, rather than dog with bone or basket.

For the beginner's version of this game players name the item and see if it matches the other player's item. Or they ask a simple question such as: "I've got a brush, what have you got?" "I've got a book."

For an intermediate version players say a sentence about their item as a clue, such as, "You use it to do your hair." Each player goes round saying a sentence to the other players until everyone has a partner.

For the advanced version players guess whether the other item matches theirs by asking questions about it without naming the item. Miming is not allowed. A question for a brush could be, "Is your item to do with hair?" You might want to give the class some ideas of questions before getting started.

For example:
Is it part of a human body?
Is it something an animal has?
Is it something an animal/human would use?
Is it large or small?
Would a person use it in the morning?
Would a person use it to clean their teeth?
Is it edible / something we would eat?
Can you __________ with it?

Language ideas

Use this with any language. For example:

1. To drill the verb to be and professions, she's a, he's a, and places of work give out one set of cards of people doing jobs and another set of the places they work such as a doctor and a hospital, a gardener and a park.

2. Passive tense example: Give out cards with vampires, werewolves and dinosaurs, or other baddies that the children know. The children ask, "Were you bitten by a dinosaur?" The reply, "I was bitten by a werewolf". This may not be appropriate in your country. It is just an example to show how to adapt language according to your needs.

3. Use with the riddles or proverbs provided at the end of this book. Cut the riddles in half and let students find the other part of their riddle.

4. Use with metaphors, jokes, sentences and even short dialogues. Split any kind of text in two or more parts and let the students find the pieces.

Fizz Buzz

Category: Speaking
Group size: Small group game
Level: Beginner to Intermediate
Materials: None
Age: 6 to adult

Pace: Wake up

Have players sit in a circle of up to 12 people. If you have too many people in the circle the game rapidly becomes dull. It is better to have two circles with your best student in charge of the second circle.

The first player says 1, the next says 2 and the next says 3, and so on. Go round the circle once like so children understand. A demonstration is worth a thousand words. Next add in an element; every time the number 2 comes up, or a number with 2 in it (such as 12, 20, 22 or 26), the player must say FIZZ instead of the number. For example:

1 FIZZ 3 4 5 6 7 8 9 10 11 FIZZ 13 14 15 16 17 18 19 FIZZ FIZZ FIZZ etc. until 30, then 31, FIZZ, 33 etc.

Once the group have mastered this idea to some degree throw in another element, such as any number with a 5 in it becomes BUZZ. This would give:

1 FIZZ 3 4 BUZZ 6 7 8 9 10 11 FIZZ 13 14 BUZZ 16 etc.

If you want to make things really complicated say that any number which can be divided by 2 or 5 is a FIZZ BUZZ. This is for older children and adults or it would be too slow to be fun.

Other language ideas

Use this fun game to revise vocabulary, for example: Using animal vocabulary have a rule where any animal ending with an O is followed by FIZZ, and any animal ending with an E is followed by BUZZ, any animal ending with a T is followed by FIZZ BUZZ. A round might look like this:

Tiger, Rhino, FIZZ, Lion, Elephant, FIZZ BUZZ, Duck, Ant, FIZZ BUZZ, Bird, Crocodile, BUZZ, etc.

This game is tricky and it is useful to precede it with a game like Brainstorm, or Ping-pong beforehand to refresh everyone's memory of animal vocabulary, write it all on the board and leave it there as a reference during the game. Write the chosen letters on the board as a reference too, in this example:

Ends with O = Fizz
Ends with E = Buzz
Ends with T = Fizz Buzz

An easier version would be to play with any vocabulary rather than limiting the students to a theme. The above idea still applies where a word ending in a given letter is followed by FIZZ or BUZZ.

Flashcard Chase

Category: Listening with optional speaking
Group size: Small group to small class
Level: Beginner to lower intermediate
Materials: Flashcards
Age: 4 to 12
Pace: Wake up

Thanks go to Tracy England in Spain for suggesting this game to me. Tracy plays this with six to eight children per circle. A significant amount of space is needed so this is not appropriate for the average classroom as children could injure themselves on the desks in their enthusiasm.

How to Play

Participants stand in a circle and the teacher numbers them from 1 to 6 or 8. Each participant is given 2 flash cards. The teacher names a flashcard first and then immediately calls out two numbers. The participants with those numbers run around the outside of the circle looking and trying to take the flash cards named by the teacher. Those in the circle hold up their cards so those running round the outside can see and take them.

This game is ideal with 6-10s, though it is also fine to use it gently with younger ones. Older and more advanced students can use it for practising verbs and tenses. Make it more challenging by asking the participant who wins the card to make a sentence with it. If the sentence given is correct, he/she wins the card. If not, the card is replaced in the game and the game continues. The teacher distributes more flashcards as necessary so that every pupils has at least one.

Flip a Card and Variants

Category: Speaking
Group size: Small group table top game
Level: Beginner to Advanced
Materials: Playing cards
Age: 6 to adult
Pace: Calm

This game is good for vocabulary revision and sentence construction. Assign two letters of the alphabet for each playing card and write this on the board. For example the Ace can be letters A and B, the 2, letters C and D, the King would correspond to the letters Y and Z and so on. There are 13 playing cards and 26 letters of the alphabet so each card will correspond to two letters.

Students play in small groups and each group has a deck of playing cards shuffled and placed face down in a pile on the table or floor. The first player turns over a card and says a word that starts with one of the two letters matched with that card. If successful the student keeps that card as a point. Students continue playing until there are no more cards in the deck.

Collaborative variant: Playing with a time limit means this can be a collaborative game too. Each group of students is a team working against the other groups. Within the given time limit students endeavour to win as many cards as possible from the deck. Students write the words down that they come up with as the game is played to prevent them from cheating.

Intermediate variant: Here students turn over several cards and say or write a sentence using words beginning with the given letters. This sentence construction may be done rigidly following a given grammatical structure or it may be used for general language revision.

For example a student turns over three playing cards, which correspond to the letters A or B, G or H and S or T. If required to use the past simple tense with these letter options examples are: Adam hated soccer, or, Beth got a tie. If allowed to make up any sentence freely examples are: Aunty goes shopping. Brigit has teeth.

For variations allow extra words to be added in the sentence to allow the students to be more creative. You may also allow the words starting with the 'playing card' letters to be placed in the sentence in any order.

Forfeits

Forfeits are not punishments for bad behaviour. They are supposed to be fun and enjoyable. If a student hates doing press ups avoid giving that student that particular forfeit. Below are ideas for forfeits to use in many games. Giving a forfeit is a useful way to 'penalise' a student for an error without making them sit out of the game. Students can do forfeits individually or as a group. The best way to get forfeits your class enjoy is to ask each pupil to come up with three funny forfeits for homework. This will give you lots of great ideas that appeal to your students. Collect them in and add them to your list for future use in games.

- Name a picture flashcard
- Make a sentence or a question using the target language
- Ask a friend any question in English
- Name three things you like
- Answer a question the teacher asks such as, "Do you have a sister?"
- Hold an orange under your chin and pass it to a neighbour
- Walk about holding an orange under your chin
- Walk about with an orange between your knees
- Balance a ball on your head for three seconds
- Bounce a ball ten times and count to ten
- Bounce a ball saying 10, 20, 30 etc. up to 100

- Say your name backwards. You may need to write the name out for the student.
- Write your name in the air with a body part such as your head, your elbow or even your bottom!
- Do a silly dance or sing a song
- Pretend to be a chicken, pig, dog, cat, lion, tiger or a snake
- Count to 10 or from 13 to 21.
- Yawn until you make someone else yawn
- Do a sum such as 70 minus 60
- Pretend to be a model and walk the catwalk
- Pretend to be Spiderman
- Fight and be killed by Darth Vader with your light sabre but only if your class know about Star Wars, otherwise replace with their latest villains and heroes.
- Hop round the room holding one foot with your hand as long (as there is space to do so without a risk of injury).
- Pretend to be a dying fly
- Perform a doggy action such as wag your tail, beg, bark
- Say a tongue twister (see Tongue Twisters for ideas)
- Try to stand on your head (probably not very appropriate for most classrooms!)
- Make someone laugh
- Limbo under a stick
- Walk across the room on your knees
- Stand on one leg and do not smile for ten seconds
- Try and make someone else laugh in ten seconds
- Pull a funny face
- Have two or more children buzz like bees and see who can buzz the longest without taking a breath
- Look at someone and do not smile for a full minute.
- Say a sentence about kangaroos, or elephants, or any other topic.
- Intermediates say 2 or 3 sentences about a topic
- Advanced students give a one-minute talk about a topic

Gorilla

Category: Speaking – vocabulary revision
Group size: Small group and large class variant
Level: Beginner to Intermediate
Materials: Picture flashcards
Age: 4 to 10
Pace: Wake up

Thank you Caleb Zimmerman, who emailed me this super game that he made up as a variant to Find the Pairs Memory Game, where students turn over two cards to try to find a matching pair.

Small Group Version

The small group variant is a combination of Find the Pairs and British Bulldog. You need space.

1. Put one desk at the back of the class and move all the others to the side of the room.
2. All students place their hands on the one desk at the back of the class.
3. On top of the desk are two identical sets of about eight vocabulary words (e.g. 2 fire fighters, 2 police officers, 2 doctors, 2 cooks). The cards are turned face-down.
4. The first student turns over a card and everyone chants the English word 3 times in unison. Then the student turns over a second card, hoping for an identical picture. The group again chants the word on the second card. If the student gets a match, the cards stay face up. If they do not match they are turned back over.
5. The second student does the same, and the third, and so on...
6. Several cards have a picture of an angry gorilla on them. If a student turns over a gorilla card you call out "gorilla" and all students run to the front of the room. If they make it to the board before you catch them, they are safe. If you catch any students, they sit out for one round or do a forfeit.

Simplified Small Group Variant

Forget the matching game and simply go through your stack of flashcards having students name them as above. If the gorilla card comes up students get chased to the board.

This game works best if you really get into your role as a gorilla and pretend to be furiously angry if all the students make it to the board before you catch them.

Large Class Version

To use this game in a typical classroom the teacher is at the front and students are at the back. The teacher holds up a flashcard and the students say the appropriate word, phrase or question. For example: picture of fish, students response is, "Do you like fish?" Then when it's the Gorilla, swap places, the teacher runs to the back and the children run to the front. Continue changing places each time the gorilla appears. Whomever you tag or touch has to do the angry monkey dance, which is a count to three, and then stand up and pound your chest while roaring. If you do it too it will help the shy ones.

If any kind of running is a no-go in your classroom replace that with the children getting down under their desks before the teacher can touch one of them, or a similar variant that does not involve organised chaos!

Go to the Vocab

Category: Speaking - giving commands and naming vocabulary
Group size: Small groups only - needs floor space
Level: Beginner to Lower Intermediate
Materials: None
Age: 4 to 12
Pace: Wake up

Lay out a course of vocabulary pictures or objects on the floor. Have a matching set of pictures or words in a hat. Player A pulls a word or picture out of the hat and tells his or her team to go to that object or picture in the course. Player A continues to pull all the words out of the hat and sends his or her team to those objects until the hat is empty.

To include more vocabulary vary the verbs you use such as "hop to the pencil", "run to the hat".

Regarding organisation, with a small group all students can run to the picture called together, racing each other. With bigger groups split them up and take turns so that you do not have too many children running at one time to prevent chaos and collisions.

Grandmother's Footsteps Adaptation

Category: Speaking
Group size: 4 to a large class
Level: Beginner to Intermediate
Materials: None
Age: 4 to 12
Pace: Wake up

This is an adaptation of the children's playground game. One of your students is grandma, down at the front, facing away from the class. Grandma asks the class to repeat certain words or phrases and at any time can raise her arms above her head as a signal, and spin around to try to catch someone moving.

For example, Grandma says, "Do you like apples?" The class creep forward while Grandma is asking the question and reply "Yes I do". While the class are replying Grandma spins around and tries to catch someone moving. Grandma then turns back to face the wall and asks, "Do you like pears?" Let a student be Grandma since it's probably not prudent for you to spend too much time with your back to the class, in case the naughty ones decide to get up to something!

Grandma can also give commands such as move to the right, look behind you, look up, look down and touch your nose.

Guess the Action

Category: Speaking - good for present and past continuous
Group size: 2 to 40
Level: Beginner to Intermediate
Materials: Picture or word flashcards
Age: 4 to 12
Pace: Wake up

How to play - present continuous and/or vocabulary

Divide the class into two teams. Show Team 1 a picture of an action or a word flashcard. Team 1 mime that action and Team 2 have to guess what they are doing.

How to play - past continuous and/or vocabulary

Divide the class into two teams. Team 1 face the wall while you show Team 2 an action which they mime until you say FREEZE. Team 2 now freeze in their positions, Team 1 turn around and have to guess what Team 1 was doing before freezing.

Organisation

With thirty children or more consider splitting the class into two sets of two teams so that smaller groups of children work together to allow more speaking opportunity. Give a different activity to the two teams acting and let them work simultaneously. Each child in the team must make one guess. Every correct guess earns a point for that team - that way you have a valid excuse to get all the children to use the target language.

Guess the Word A

Category: Writing and speaking
Group size: 2 to 30
Level: Beginner to Intermediate

Materials: Pen and paper or the class board
Age: 6 to Adult
Pace: Calm

Have a player come up to the board and write down the letters you spell out. Take your time in between letters, as the idea is that students guess what word you are spelling out. Divide the class into teams and encourage the children to call out any word at all regardless of the fact that you may only have written one letter so far. As an incentive award one point for any word that could have been correct and five points for the actual correct word. For example if your word is CHOCOLATE it starts with C so a child who calls out CAT wins a point. Award five points when someone calls out CHOCOLATE. This is a good game to play prior to Brainstorm, Fizz Buzz, Ping Pong, or any of the more demanding games that require extensive vocabulary.

For an easy version, use words from a theme such as food. Use random words for more advanced players with larger vocabulary. Give clues if you need to or if no guesses are forthcoming add another letter to move on.

Guess the Word B

Category: Writing and speaking
Group size: 2 to 40
Level: Beginner to Intermediate
Materials: Pen and paper or the class board
Age: 6 to Adult
Pace: Calm

Play as described above and involve more people at once by making each column of people in the class a team, with one child from each team at the board. The one at the front has a series of words, which can all belong to a theme for beginners, but can be totally random for advanced players. The person at the front starts to write out the word, but is only allowed to write out the first 4 letters, then his or her team has to guess the word. As soon as someone on the team guesses the word correctly the one at the front writes out the first four letters of the second word, and so on until all the words have been guessed. The idea is to be the first team to guess all the words. Give out different words for each team in this game, as the teams will hear the other teams calling out words. A quick way to prepare is to have each team write down 5 or 6 words for another team to guess.

GAMES H-J

Hangman

Category: Spelling and speaking
Group size: Pair work or small groups
Level: Beginner to Intermediate
Materials: Pen and paper or the class board
Age: 6 to 12
Pace: Calm

This is the classic hangman game of old. Decide on a word and write up the number of letters in that word with dashes. E.g. if the word were Dinosaur you would write up _ _ _ _ _ _ _ _. The other players have to guess what the word is and they do this by naming the letters of the alphabet.

If they name a letter which is in the word, for example in this case the letter N, then you fill it into the blank: _ _ n _ _ _ _ _. If however a letter is named which is not part of the word, such as the letter E in this case, then you start to draw the "hangman". The drawing represents a man being hung from a noose. The idea is that the word must be guessed before the man is hung. The hangman is drawn in eleven strokes as shown below.

For something less murderous make up your own little sketch such as a cowboy's face, the nose being the last thing to go on. A non-violent alternative of a train is shown below. The last thing to be drawn is the smoke, which means that you have missed the train if you have not guessed the word by then. Draw this in eleven strokes also, first the round face, left eye, right eye, mouth, the whole body as the fifth stroke, each wheel one after the other, the chimney as the tenth stroke, and finally the smoke.

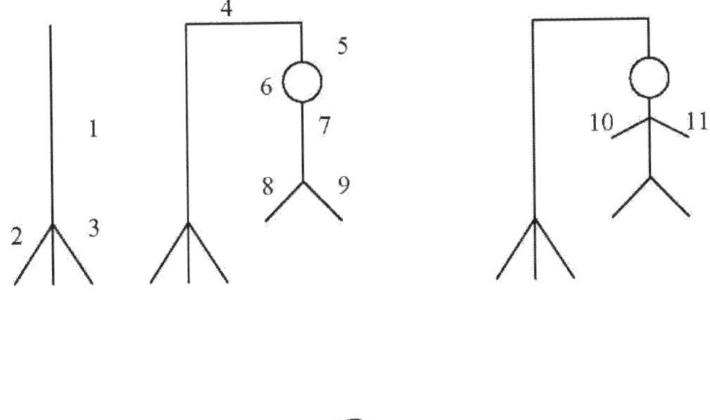

Hangman Variant

Category: Speaking
Group size: Pair work or small groups
Level: Beginner to Intermediate
Materials: Pen and paper or the class board
Age: 6 to 12
Pace: Calm

Using the same drawings as above play Hangman to do more than say letters and spell words. Here is an example using clothing words: You, or a class member stand up at the board with a picture of a person in various clothes. The class have to guess what the person is wearing before you finish the hangman.

First tell them if it is a man or a woman. If it is a man your group members ask questions like "Is he wearing a shirt?" If he is wearing a shirt you draw it. If he is not wearing a shirt you start the hangman. You could turn this into a general guessing game using multiple question forms where the class have to guess what is on a given picture. The object or activity depicted must be guessed before the hangman is completed.

Happy Families

Category: Speaking
Group size: Small groups of 3 to 5 players
Level: Beginner to Lower Intermediate
Materials: Happy Families sets
Age: 4 to 12
Pace: Calm

Materials

For this game you need sets of Happy Families cards. You can buy these in toy stores or make them. There are printable happy family sets included with the flashcards here:
www.teachingenglishgames.com/esl-flashcards

How to play

Each group shuffles and deals out one set of families. The players have to take care not to show their cards to the others, and the 4 to 6 year olds can't generally do this but it doesn't matter! In turn each player asks any other player for a member of one of the families. If the player asked has the family member he or she must hand it over. If he or she does not have it that is the end of the turn, and the next player in the circle asks for a family member. The idea is to be the first to collect a whole family.

Language ideas

Use this to drill either "Have you got? Yes I have" or "Do you have? Yes I do".

Have you got Mr. Smith? / Mrs., Miss, Master
Have you got daddy Smith? / mummy, brother, sister
Have you got father Alien? / mother, son, daughter
Do you have?
I would like Mr. Bunny please.
Please give me brother Piglet.
Can I have sister Singer?
Please could I have Mother Swan?

Before you play Happy Families your players need to recognise and know the vocabulary for all of the family members involved. Play some of the other games such as Jump the Line, Rapid reaction, or Find the pairs memory game with the Happy Family cards first to familiarise everyone with the characters in the families.

Head to Head

Category: Listening
Group size: 4 to 30 or pair work
Level: Beginner
Materials: Optional picture flashcards or objects
Age: 4 to 12
Pace: Excitable

Players pair up and form two circles, one player on the inside circle and the other on the outer circle. One player stands in the middle of the circle. Play some music or have the group sing a song or chant a rhyme while the outer circle rotates one way and the inner circle goes the other. When the music stops call out a command such as Head to Head! The players must find their partner and stand head to head. The one in the middle tries to get catch someone before they have found their partner and the new odd one out goes in the middle.

Other ideas for commands are; hand to knee, nose to nose, eye to eye, cheek to cheek, foot to foot, mouth to ear, head to toe, hand in hand, back to back, ear to ear, hand to ear, back to front, foot to bottom, heel to toe, shoulder to shoulder, finger to finger, finger to nose etc.

Variants for larger classes, or if you have no space

If it is too boisterous with an odd one out in the middle then suppress that and just have the children race to find their partner and get into the required position.

If even that creates too much chaos for your liking, then the children just go head to head with the nearest person when the music stops rather than rushing around looking for the original partner. This alternative is practical if you have too much furniture in your class to make circles. In that case have people walking slowly and randomly around the class, between the desks, and go head to head with the nearest person when you say so.

If even this version is too chaotic just put your class into pairs and have them assume the position you describe.

Language ideas aside from body parts

Aside from body parts play the game in the way described above but give the children a selection of picture or word flashcards. Call out combinations when the music stops and the children with those pictures pair up according to your instructions. For example you might call out, "bananas and apples, oranges and pears". The bananas and apples pair up, as do the oranges and pears. Children with other picture cards do nothing. Start the music again and call out a different combination of pictures.

Hidden Picture A

Category: Speaking
Group size: 2 to a class
Level: Beginner to Intermediate
Materials: A piece of card with slits or holes in it.
Age: 6 to 12
Pace: Calm to Wake up

Materials

Take a piece of card and make some slits or holes in it. For young children make bigger holes. Make thin slits for older children. The bigger the hole or the wider the slit the easier it is to see the picture underneath. Ideally use dark card so that they are not see-through.

How to play

The card with slits or holes is placed over a picture so that only parts of that picture are visible. Players have to guess what the picture is behind the card.

Divide your group into two teams, hold or stick up a hidden picture saying, "Ready, steady, go!" and both teams attempt to name the picture first.

Small group version

If you have a small group have opposite numbers of each team play each other. If you play as a whole team then be careful that it is not always the same players giving the answers, while others do not get a chance because they are not quick enough. One way around that is to have the quickest ones hold up the card. A way to handle it with pair work is to put the brightest children together so they play against each other.

Class version

Make teams, one team per row of chairs or table. Each team has a referee who is neutral. With 30 players you could have 5 teams of 5 players and a referee. Place the hidden pictures at the front, one set per team. Each referee also has a set of the same pictures and stands at the back of the class, keeping his or her pictures hidden from the others.

Player 1 from each team runs up to the hidden pictures for his or her team at the front. As soon as player 1 has identified one of the pictures he or she calls it out to the team referee at the back. If the item called out is correct player 1 reveals the item named and sits down.

Player 2 then goes up and names one of the remaining hidden items, calls it out to the referee, and so on. After the first round change the referees over. If the player calls out the wrong item it is the next person's turn. With younger children it doesn't matter if you have re-peat items in each team and make it so easy and obvious that everyone succeeds in identifying the pictures.

Hidden Picture B

Category: Writing
Group size: 2 to a class
Level: Beginner to Intermediate
Materials: Easy to make. A piece of card with slits or holes
Age: 6 to 12
Pace: Calm

In this version spread up to 20 hidden pictures around the classroom and on your signal the everyone freely identifies each picture. If you have no room for children to move around then display several pictures on the walls or board where children can see them from their desks and write down the items.

Hide and Seek Prepositions

Category: Speaking
Group size: 2 to 30
Level: Beginner to Intermediate
Materials: Pebbles or other small items
Age: 4 to 12
Pace: Excitable

Small group version

Hide pebbles or items around the room. Players search for the pebbles, and make a note of where they find them. At the end players say where the pebbles or items are, for example: There's one under Sarah's book. There's one by the door.

Class version

Divide the class into two, one half have a pebble to hide, and stay near the hiding place. The other half go up to a member of the opposite team, search for the pebble, and can only claim it if they can tell the person who hid it where it is in English.

Large class version

Go through some possible hiding places in your classroom. Ideas would be in your pocket, under your book, under the table, on your chair, in your pencil case, on your green book, in your bag, in your hand, in your left hand and so on. In pairs pupil A hides an item while pupil B looks away. Pupil B must then find the item by asking questions such as "Is it in your pocket?" Play once and swap over.

Higher or Lower

Category: Speaking
Group size: Pair work to a large class
Level: Beginner

Materials: One or more packs of playing cards
Age: 4 to 12
Pace: Calm

Class version

If working with the whole class turn over a playing card and read the number out loud. With all players standing, and divided into two teams, everyone decides whether the next card will be higher or lower than the previous one. Those who think it will be higher say "higher" and point towards the ceiling. All those who think it will be lower say "lower" and point towards the floor. Turn over the next card and read it out. Those who were wrong are out and sit down. Continue for three rounds and then count up how many are standing from each team. Start a new round.

Pair work version

In pairs each pair has a pack of playing cards or number cards. Each player states whether they think the next card will be higher or lower, if correct the player keeps the card and the idea is to collect as many cards as possible. Where there is a tie, i.e. if both players say "higher", then the card remains in the pile. The next time one of the pair wins they take the whole pile of unclaimed cards. Practise numbers by having a player name the card that is turned over each time.

Language ideas: Numbers and comparatives

To work with the higher numbers say that each number is x10 or x100 its face value. So 6 would become 60 or 600.

This is also an ideal game to practise comparatives such as "5 is higher than 4", "3 is lower than 10", or "more than," "less than" and "the same as".

A variant on this game is to use sets of picture cards. Here is an example with animals: Each time a card is turned over players guess whether the next one will be bigger or smaller, (in real life, not in the picture). Other examples that spring to mind are people, who can be taller, shorter, thinner, fatter, more intelligent than or prettier, etc. Use types of transport, which can be faster or slower. If you do not have any pictures use word flash cards instead.

Hot Potato

Category: Speaking
Group size: Small group to a large class
Level: Beginner to Advanced
Materials: One or more potatoes or similar. Optional blindfold.
Age: 4 to 12
Pace: Wake up

Sit the children in a circle with one player blindfolded or eyes closed in the middle. If you have no space for a circle leave the children sitting at their desks and they can pass the potatoes from their seats. The players pass the potato round as quickly as they can until the player in the middle calls out "Hot Potato!"

The player holding the potato at this moment has to do a forfeit. See Forfeits for ideas. With a big circle or class have two or more potatoes passed round at intervals of a few people, to keep everyone actively occupied. In this case all those holding a potato do the forfeit together.

Large class variant

Use this game as an excuse to frequently go over a song or a rhyme. You'll want to have introduced the song in a previous lesson. You'll need at least one potato to every six students. Establish the route the potatoes will take around the class and pass the potatoes along it by way of demonstration. Start the song and while pupils sing they pass the potatoes. Somewhere during the song, unexpectedly, you make a loud noise or clap. The class instantly stop singing and all pupils with potatoes do a forfeit.

Language ideas

Singing, chanting or saying a rhyme as the potato is passed round, or, with a small to medium group the person in the middle can ask the people caught holding potatoes a question, and if they answer it correctly they do not have to do the forfeit.

A more advanced idea is for each player to say a word beginning with a certain letter as the potato is passed round. A word cannot be used twice. If pupils cannot think of a word they hold the potato while thinking - increasing their chance of being caught with it.

A variant of this is to say any word as long as it is part of a given theme such as an animal, a profession, a place such as bank or supermarket, a country or a colour. After each round change the theme or the letter.

Another variant for players to think of a word that begins with the last letter of the previous word. If player 1 says "bat", player 2 can say any word beginning with "T", such as "tree", player 3 must now think of any word beginning with the letter "E" and so on. Allow the repetition of words to help keep the game flowing and pass around several potatoes around at once.

I Spy

Category: Speaking
Group size: Pair work to groups of up to 10
Level: Beginner to Intermediate
Materials: Pictures on the walls are useful
Age: 4 to 12
Pace: Calm

This is the classic game that so many of us have played on a long car journey during which we drove the adults spare asking if we were nearly there yet, barely had we left the house. One player looks around the room, garden, or whichever environment you are in, and secretly chooses an item. You could have them tell you the item to prevent them changing their minds mid-game, which does have a tendency of happening!

The player then says "I spy with my little eye, something beginning with ___" (whichever letter of the alphabet the item they have decided on begins with). For example if the child has decided on a bag they will say, "I spy with my little eye something beginning with B". The other players then have to guess the item by calling out possibilities such as "book" or "bicycle". In a classroom situation put pictures up on the walls to enrich vocabulary opportunities. This is a particularly good end of term revision game.

Children can play in pairs or in small groups. It can quickly become dull if played as a large class as children can too easily drift off and stop participating.

Jackpot

Category: Easy speaking
Group size: Small group to class of about 30
Level: Beginner
Materials: Pictures on the board or flashcards
Age: 4 to 12
Pace: Calm

Thanks to the teacher who emailed me this game. The teacher chooses 6 students who go to the board. The teacher explains the students are going to practise vocabulary such as: numbers from 1 to 20 or the alphabet. The first child says "1, 2, 3" the next one "4" and the third one will say "5, 6, 7", the fourth one says "8". The teacher has set a "lucky number" on the board previously which will give one point to the child or team that student represents, let's say "20". As the children get close to reaching that number they start to get excited.

To use this with vocabulary other than numbers or the alphabet have pictures up on the board, or hold up flashcards. The lucky word can be written up on the board for all to see.

Joker

Category: Speaking - question and answer game
Group size: Small group card game
Level: Beginner to Intermediate
Materials: Pack of playing cards
Age: 4 to 12
Pace: Calm

Deal out half a pack of playing cards including the jokers to a small group of up to six children. The players must not look at their cards but place them face down. Ask player 1 a question. Player 1 answers and turns over a playing card from his or her pile. If the answer is correct the card is taken out of the game. If the answer is incorrect the card is placed in a pile in the middle. Continue by asking the next child a question. When a child turns up the joker that child must collect all the discarded cards from the pile in the middle, UNLESS he or she has answered the question correctly, in which case the joker is taken out of the game. You may like to add in a couple of extra jokers from another pack.

Complicate the game for variety with older children. For example you could say that any child turning up an ace may keep it as a "life-saver" against a potential future joker.

If you have well behaved children who will stay on task let them play in small groups. In this case the teacher cannot ask the questions for every group. Instead provide a set of cards or pieces of paper with questions. Put each of your best students in charge of a group. Children can call on the teacher to arbitrate and check answers if they are not sure.

Language ideas

Use any question forms you like. Use the same question form over and over for a simple level and mix up various types of questions for revision games or for more advanced levels.

Jump the Line

Category: Listening
Group size: 2 to a big class
Level: Beginner to Intermediate
Materials: Picture or word flashcards and/or a classroom board
Age: 4 to 12
Pace: Wake up

This game is ideal to present new vocabulary. Ideally play in a space on the floor. Designate an imaginary line and place pictures or words either side of that line, to the left and to the right. In a class with no room draw a vertical line down the middle of the board and stick up or draw pictures either side of the line. Call out the items and players jump to the right or to the left depending on the location of the picture in relation to the line.

If your children are stuck on benches with no room to move they can make arm gestures instead of jumping.

Language ideas

As well as presenting new vocabulary use this game to familiarise players with a grammatical structure by repeating the same sentence each time, with a different noun represented by the picture or word on the board. Call out actress, singer, businessman, if you are learning the professions for the first time. Call out a sentence such as, "I'd like to be an actress" or, "I'd like to be a singer" to revise professions and introduce the conditional. Do not introduce new vocabulary and a new structure in the same game.

Jungle Treasure

Category: Speaking
Group size: Groups of 8 to 20 players or so - space needed
Level: Beginner to Intermediate
Materials: Treasure and optional magic wands

Age: 4 to 12
Pace: Wake up, possibly excitable

The group make a jungle of people, stretching out their feet and arms like plants. Pupils' hands and feet touch the bodies of the people next to them so that there is no way through. The treasure is placed in the middle of the jungle. Two at a time, or in threes or fours if you have a larger group, the players, each starting from a different entry point, have to get through the jungle to the treasure. They can only get through by asking the plants to move, and the plants can only move one body part each. The player has to get through the jungle without touching any of the plants, and make it to the treasure before the other players, but ignore this rule if with younger players since it is too difficult. The idea is also for the plants not to be touched by the player, so it becomes a cooperative game not a competitive one.

If your group is overly competitive add enough treasure for every player to find some, which is recommended anyway with the younger players who can otherwise be quite devastated not to have any treasure!

Decide on the magic words to get the plants to move or use short dialogues like:

Player: Excuse me please

Plants: Oh, Sorry! The plant makes way for the treasure seeker.

OR Player: Please move your left arm (practise body parts)

Plants: Yes of course

OR Player: With my magic wand I move your leg (touches leg with hand or wand)

Language variant

To drill a vocabulary theme each plant has a specific magic word that opens the passage to the treasure. For example each plant could be an item of clothing. The player trying to reach the treasure names clothing items until he or she hits on the magic one for that plant.

GAMES K-M

Keep a Straight Face

Category: Speaking - question practice
Group size: 2 to 40
Level: Beginner to Intermediate
Materials: None
Age: 4 to 12
Pace: Calm to wake up

With a small class put one student on the spot at the front and the others in a line or circle around the student. The students think up questions to ask the student on the spot and the first student to have a question ready asks it. The student on the spot replies. From now on all questions must be answered with this same reply without the student on the spot laughing or smiling. So the first question might be: Where do you live. The reply will be something like: Hong Kong. The next question might be: What's your name. The reply must be: Hong Kong. If the student on the spot smiles or has any expression other than a dead-pan straight face then he or she is off the spot and goes into the line or circle and another student has a turn on the spot. Rotate turns on the spot.

With a big class you will have to have two or three groups playing simultaneously otherwise there will be long delays in taking turns asking questions. Encourage students to ask different questions but allow beginners to repeat questions that have been asked already.

Glenda Rodriguez contributed the fixed reply 'Grandpa's pooh pooh pants' to the game because understandably her young pupils find it hilarious, obviously don't use this if it is not to your taste or acceptable in your culture. Where do you live? Grandma's pooh pooh pants. What's for lunch? Grandma's pooh pooh pants.

Kidnap

Category: Speaking
Group size: Large group to a very large class
Level: Beginner to Intermediate
Materials: Picture flashcards
Age: 4 to 12
Pace: Wake up

Teach this game in stages and demonstrate it. The first time you use it play just passing pictures as described in the section below entitled 'The play'. When students successfully complete that part of the game add in the 'kidnap' papers, as described below. This breaks the learning of the game up into two simple stages. Teachers have reported back that children adore this game so it is worth learning and of course you may re-use it regularly for different vocabulary, grammar and revision.

Set up

Divide the class into teams, which do not have to be exactly even. Draw or stick vocabulary pictures on the board. Tell each child to copy one of these pictures and make sure that all the pictures are being drawn more or less equally. One way to do this is to number the pictures on the board and then count round the children. The children draw the picture their number corresponds to. Children then write their team name or letter on the picture. Use words instead of pictures if you are practising a sentence with a target structure, but if you are working on vocabulary pictures are much more effective.

While children are drawing write out the team names or letters in a column on the board and allocate nine lives to each team horizontally. Each time a team loses a life rub one off the board.

TEAM	LIVES							
The Pixels	1	2	3	4	5	6	7	8	9
Vampires	1	2	3	4	5	6	7	8	9
The Dudes	1	2	3	4	5	6	7	8	9
The Geeks	1	2	3	4	5	6	7	8	9
The Ghosts	1	2	3	4	5	6	7	8	9

By now each student has a piece of paper with a picture on it. Make sure students have written their team name or letter on the paper. Ask students to each take a second piece of paper and one pupil from each team only draws a square on it, pressing lightly so the pencil line does not show through the paper. The other pupils leave their paper blank. Everyone now folds this second piece of paper in half.

Now all students pass the folded papers around until no one knows who has the papers with the square on. Your pupils look secretly at their folded paper to see if they have the square, and don't tell anyone if they do.

The play

Now you are ready to play. Call out one of the words such as "bananas". All those with a banana picture hold up their hands. Pick one and that person stands up and is the collector of all the banana pictures. Do the same for another picture, such as milk. You now have two students standing, one who will collect in all the bananas and the other all the milk.

Give the word or sentence that is to be repeated on passing a picture. A picture can only be passed when this word or phrase is spoken otherwise it's cheating. Use repetition of the given vocabulary, or short sentences such as "I like bananas" if passing the bananas, or "I like milk" if passing the milk.

Use whispering or murmuring to keep a lid on the noise. Anyone talking or saying anything other than the given vocabulary or phrase loses a life for his or her team or rub out one of the lives you drew on the board earlier.

Anyone with a banana picture passes his or her paper along the line in the direction of the collector, while the milk simultaneously makes its way to the milk collector. Everyone passing a picture must say the given word or phrase to the person he or she hands it to. The paper takes the most direct line towards the collector and no one can be missed out in the line of flight so to speak. Alternatively have a rule that the paper cannot travel diagonally but can only go up or across rows. Use whatever works best for your classroom configuration so that the maximum number of people have to pass the paper to include as many students as possible.

After a few goes ask if anyone has not yet had a go at all. Specify that for the next round the paper must go via those people who have not had a turn, and ask them to stand up so they can be identified.

The 'kidnap' papers

Now here's the snag! Those with the papers with a square can kidnap a picture if it comes their way, and take it out of the game. If anyone succeeds in doing this they shout out "Kidnapped!" and tell you the team letter on the paper they have intercepted. This is the equivalent of a member of that team being taken hostage and that team loses a life. With older children they can also write their name on their paper, along with their drawing and team letter, so that specific class members are kidnapped. (The younger ones won't really like this so for them keep it general.)

Continue to play using the other words. Have a blank paper swap every couple of rounds so that the square 'kidnap' papers can secretly circulate. At the end you see which team has the most lives.

Use this game for any language. It's great because everyone has a chance to speak and drill themselves in the given words or phrases while having fun.

Ladders Basic Version

Category: Speaking
Group size: 8 to 40
Level: Beginner to Intermediate
Materials: None or Picture flashcards
Age: 4 to 12
Pace: Wake up

This is a running game and nothing to do with the board game Snakes and Ladders. You need a big space to play. As children we played it at Scouts in the village hall. Divide the class into two and have pupils sit on the floor opposite a partner in two lines with legs stretched out and feet touching the partner's feet opposite. The pattern made on the floor by all the players is similar to a ladder, with the two lines of players making up the vertical sides of the ladder and their outstretched legs being the rungs. The players must keep their legs and feet on the floor at all times so as not to trip any players up.

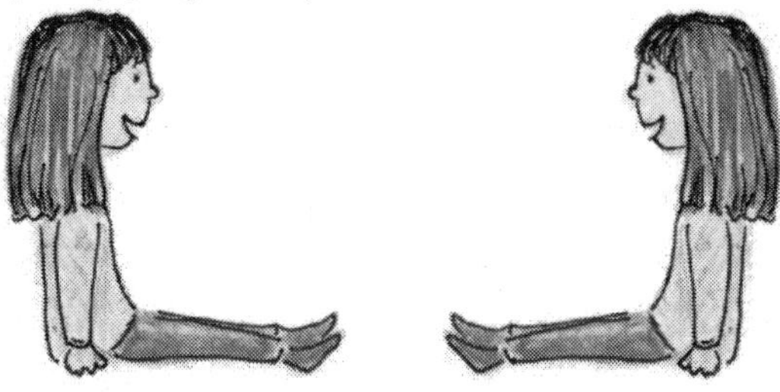

Starting at one end of the line give the first player and his partner opposite a number. The next player along and his opposite would be number 2, and the next pair number 3 until all players have a number. The player and his partner opposite have the same number and will race against each other. The children either remember their number or picture, but for the younger ones give out picture cards so they do not forget what number or picture they are.

Call out one of the numbers or the picture - for example 7 or the doctors - and pair number 7 or the doctors get up, run over the legs to the end of the line, round the pair at the end and back up through the middle of the ladder to get back to their original place and sit down. The idea is to get back to your place before your opposite number.

Ladders game example with 18 children and professions vocabulary where the plumbers get up and run through the ladder.

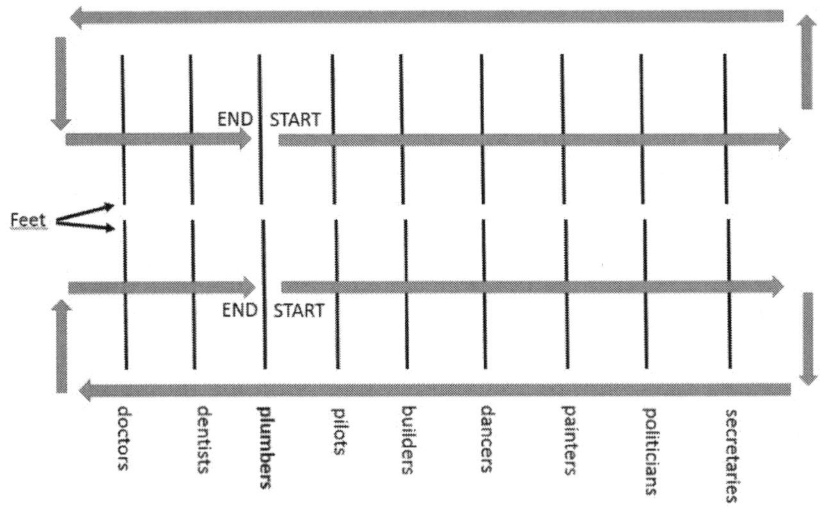

It is a good idea to match up the faster runners if possible, but if not then at least avoid putting Speedy Gonzales opposite the slowest. Use numbers or vocabulary for this game. Do be attentive to give each pair the same number of goes. An easy way of ensuring this is to have your own set of picture cards and simply work your way through it - but in random order so the players never know who will be the next pair to run.

Ladders Question and Answer

Category: Speaking

Group size: 8 to 40
Level: Beginner to Intermediate
Materials: None or picture flashcards
Age: 4 to 12
Pace: Wake up

This is played as Ladders Basic Version, the difference being that all the players ask a question of your choice in unison, to which you give a reply. For example all the players ask you "What's the weather like?" and you reply, "It's raining" or, "It's sunny" etc. Each pair has a picture card representing a type of weather, or a word card with the phrase on it.

This game is best for beginners and intermediates, but it may be used with advanced students for complex structures. Give a player a turn at calling out the answers - just watch that they do not always pick their friends to run.

Limbo

This is a fairly outrageous game. It won't be suitable for all cultures so use at your discretion. I'd use this at the end of term or the end of a class. Play some fun music while your pupils stand in line waiting to bend backwards low enough to fit under the limbo stick (broom handle, pole or stick). In order to win, the limbo master must not touch the stick or fall on the floor while limbo-ing under the stick (which is usually held by 2 people). As an alternative to the stick two children may join hands with outstretched arms to make

the stick. With larger groups you need several limbo sticks so the wait for a turn is greatly reduced.

This is an ideal game to play during a song. Children walk around the class in a chain, going under the limbo sticks whenever they come to them. Anyone touching the sticks sits down. Anyone who accidentally stops singing is out! The teacher goes around gradually lowering the sticks so that the limbo-ing becomes more and more difficult.

Use this idea as a forfeit as part of any game. Or incorporate it in to any game. For example in Relay Race the last person in line limbos under a stick. It can be inserted almost anywhere to liven up a language exchange.

Make a Sentence or a Question

Category: Speaking and writing variant
Group size: 2 to 30
Level: Beginner to Intermediate
Materials: None. Optional bells or buzzers
Age: 6 to Adult
Pace: Calm

How to play

Divide your group into teams and say a word out loud. The teams have their fingers on their bells or buzzers and as soon as they have figured out a sentence with the word in they hit their buzzer and say their sentence to get a point for their team if correct. Instead of bells or buzzers have the children knock on their desks when they have an answer ready. Allow 3 to 5 seconds to reply before other teams are allowed to jump in and use their buzzers. The best students have the job of writing up the sentences and saying whether they are correct. This prevents those students from answering everything and gives them the challenge of writing and the responsibility score-keeping.

Language ideas

This game is adaptable to any language. Practise English in a general way or be specific. To focus in on a specific linguistic structure specify that the sentence must be in a certain tense, or using a certain phrase. Here is a simple version and a complex one:

Simple example: Say different foods and the children make up sentences or questions about whether they like or dislike them.

Or hold up a picture and say, "sentence" or "question". The class or team must come up with something. For example, hold up a picture of "potatoes" and say "question", the students must think of a question with that word in it such as: "Do you like potatoes?" or "Can I have some potatoes please?" or "Are there any potatoes?"

Complex example: To work on if + past perfect with the perfect conditional the sentence must contain a phrase like "If I had wanted".

If the word is "mother" the player makes up a sentence such as "If I had wanted mother to do it I would have asked her".

If the word is "tiger" a sentence could be "If I had wanted to see a tiger I would have gone to India". And so on.

Advanced variant

A variant of this game is that with each the players come up with a sentence as part of a story they make up as the game goes along. The first to finish rings the buzzer and reads out their chosen sentence. The other team decides if it is correct grammatically and if so awards a point. To keep everyone working have every team member create his or her own sentence on hearing the word but only one is chosen to read out the sentence. Work with small teams to keep all children involved.

If the sentence is not correct the opposite team have a chance to gain a point offering one of their sentences, and if not correct you go back to the first team, or to a third team for a different sentence, and so on until you have a correct sentence which is the first line of a story.

Next write the chosen sentence on the board as a reference. Use blue pen for all correct sentences from team A, red pen from team B and so on, so you know who has contributed what to the story at the end.

With a big class an option is to draw names out of a hat at random for the sentence contribution and allow other members of the same team to correct the sentence if need be before presenting their final version. However do endeavour to keep the pace going and don't make students wait while you write on the board, but let them be working on the next sentence of the story. Alternatively have one of your students write on the board instead of you.

Making Up Stories

Category: Speaking and writing
Group size: 2 to 30
Level: Intermediate to Advanced
Materials: One bingo set or random pictures for every 3 to 6 players
Age: 8 to 12
Pace: Calm

How to play

Put your class into small groups, the smaller the better, and have them make up a story which they write as they go.

Use pictures: Give out random pictures from a cartoon or magazine and instruct the class to make up any kind of story as long as elements from those pictures are included. It does not matter if the story is plausible or far-fetched. The important thing is that the grammar and use of language is correct. Students will enjoy the challenge of making up a story using their imagination, rather than following the often dull and obvious story lines of picture composition prompts often provided in text books.

Keep a copy of any good ones, edit them and use them for reading texts. This way your reading texts are sure to appeal to your target audience!

Language and marking

Encourage students to keep it simple as the temptation is to try to write an incredible story when the language and grammar is not there yet to do so. For specific work on tenses specify the tense the story takes place in - for example it was yesterday, it is happening now, or it is someone telling the story of what they plan to do in the future.

Once they have written the story have pupils swap stories and read each other's - each group must correct any language mistakes they see, by writing out the correct version beneath the story. Each time the story is passed to another group they add any corrections they feel necessary. As far as the corrections go you may have several versions offered so go through these reading out the different versions and having the class say which one is correct. Having the class participating in the marking of work makes them focus on the details such as verb endings and those little prepositions that are so often wrong. It is a great exercise in awareness.

A follow-up game could be for a few students to come up to the front and act out one of the stories while the class have to guess which story it is.

Matching and Mirroring

Category: Listening
Group size: Any
Level: Beginner to Intermediate
Materials: None
Age: 4 to 12
Pace: Wake up

Matching and mirroring is known in the art of NLP (neuro-linguistic-programming) for its capacity to bond people together. People often subconsciously mirror each other and this shows that there is some sort of bond or connection taking place. Consciously copying each other will also create a bond, and your group will feel positive after playing this game, because they will have connected with another human being without even being aware of it.

Divide your group or class up into pairs or small groups. One person per group is the leader and the others are the mirrors. Call out things for the leader to do such as "touch their toes" or "dance rock or ballet", and the mirrors copy the particular way the leader does it. After a few goes swap the leader over and continue. Increase the difficulty of the language according to the level of your group from simple commands to more imaginative language and actions such as waving in the wind like a field of corn.

Young children are often happy acting right away, but older players may need to warm up so start conservatively and gradually give them more and more outrageous things to do.

Match Up – Writing and Speaking

Category: Writing and speaking
Group size: 8 to 40
Level: Beginner to Intermediate
Materials: None
Age: 6 to 12
Pace: Calm

How to play

Pupils write down a favourite food. Collect in the slips of paper and read them to the class. Students write each one down on a separate line. Then they go round the class asking each other, "What is your favourite food?" and writing the name of each child by the food in question. If you have a class of thirty just dictate ten favourite foods and let the children find out who the ten people are who match those food items.

Allow five minutes for pupils to ask as many people as possible in that time. Then see who has asked the most people. That should motivate the children to stay on target.

Language ideas for this game

Where the children live, such as in a white house, in a flat on the third floor, on a farm with sheep, etc. Favourite toys, favourite colour, favourite item of clothing, favourite band, favourite hobby, favourite film or cartoon character, favourite place for holidays, favourite sport, etc. Pick something the children enjoy talking about naturally then they will be more interested in finding out the match.

Miming Games

Category: Speaking
Group size: 2 to 40
Level: Beginner to Advanced
Materials: None or props if you wish
Age: 4 to 12
Pace: Wake up

How to play

Miming games can be played in pairs or small teams, where one person gets up and mimes in front of the others in their team who guess what the action is. Give everyone a turn at acting, regardless of whether they guessed the last mime or not.

Language ideas

Miming games can be adapted to a wide range of language uses such as:

Guess what they are eating: ice cream, pasta, chewy toffees, chewing gum, hot dog, chips, steak

Guess who they are in the family: mum, dad, baby, sister, brother, grandfather, great-grandmother

Guess the action: close the curtains, knock on the door, sit on the floor, stand up, see, look, run, walk, sleep, cry, sing, dance, play tennis, football

Guess the feeling: happy, sad, angry, sleepy, dreamy, tired

Guess the profession: doctor, nurse, taxi driver, schoolteacher, footballer, racing driver, farmer, opera singer, actor, clown, circus acrobat

Guess the animal: mime the animal with or without sound effects

Miming letters of the alphabet in pairs

Musical Vocabulary

Category: Listening
Group size: 2 to 30
Level: Beginners
Materials: Sets of picture cards
Age: 4 to 12
Pace: Wake up to Excitable

How to play

Spread picture cards on the floor and have the group walk or dance in a circle around the pictures to play music. Stop the music unpredictably and call out one of the picture cards, or a sentence containing one of the picture cards, such as "hamburger" or "I'd like a hamburger". The players jump on the relevant picture.

With 20 players use 3 hamburger pictures, 3 pizzas, 3 milkshakes, etc. If you allow 4 players per picture when the music stops, you'll have 8 players out in the first round. Eliminate the rest fast by allowing only 2 per picture for the next round, and then 1 per picture, so that everyone is back in playing again very soon. Adapt the rules as necessary according to your group size. Involve those who are out by having them call out the next word.

Tip: Avoid having a lot of students trying to converge on only one picture.

If you do not have music the players can circle round the pictures chanting a rhyme or singing and at the end of each verse or song the picture card is called out.

Adaptation if you have no open space

Place the picture cards on the desks. The players must touch the desk with the corresponding picture. To keep the children from banging themselves on the furniture from over-excitement use the following rule, which slows everyone right down: when walking the heel of one foot must touch the toe of the other, as you would do if you were measuring the length of a room in feet, (which by the way is something the English do).

Mystery Bag

Category: Speaking and spelling options
Group size: 2 to a class, better for small classes or groups
Level: Beginners
Materials: An opaque bag (i.e. you can't see through it)
Age: 4 to 12
Pace: Calm

Give each group a black bag containing a few mystery items. Each group must feel the items in the bag and tell you what they are for speaking, or write them on the board for spelling. You or the players write the guesses under each team. If you are using different items for each group each team can swap their bag with another group and have another feel and guess. With one to three items per bag teams continue to swap bags until they have guessed at the items in all bags. At that point have pupils open the bags and name the items.

Recruit one player per team to come up and mark the answers given, total up the points and see which team guessed the most correct items. Speaking opportunities are sentences like "It's an apple", "I think it's an apple" or "There is an apple in the bag". Use any objects you have to hand such as: pens, a rubber, a calculator, an old pair of glasses, a roll of tape, a spoon, toys such as Barbie, mini cars, an apple, an orange, a tennis ball, a ping pong ball, a plastic mug, a piece of paper, medium-sized plastic animals and dinosaurs, favourite toys such as Spiderman, or whatever is "in" at the time, etc.

Tip: Think of intriguing items combinations. For sound try nails in a metal box, sand in a plastic box or nuts in a bag. For feel try a hairbrush, a pan cleaner or a toy giraffe or elephant.

GAMES N-P

Name and Chase

Category: Speaking
Group size: 2 to 30
Level: Beginner to Lower Intermediate
Materials: Pictures
Age: 4 to 12
Pace: Wake up to Excitable

One student is the wolf at the front of the class. The teacher shows everyone including the wolf a picture card. The wolf asks a particular student; "What is it?" The wolf can try to catch the student unless the student names the picture. If the wolf catches the student they swap roles. If the wolf fails to catch anyone after a few goes bring up another student to be the wolf and pick one who has not yet been chased either to share out the participation.

This game can be used for revising vocabulary, for practising telling the time and for any kind of question and answer format.

Noughts and Crosses

Category: Speaking
Group size: Any - pair work

Level: Beginner to Lower Intermediate
Materials: Noughts and Crosses sets - see below
Age: 4 to 12
Pace: Calm

Give out or have the class make one grid per pair. A grid consists of nine pictures in three rows of three. The players need five items each to use as markers. Either give these out, pieces of uncooked pasta twists work fine, or players use their own items such as blue pen lids and red pen lids, or pen lids on one side and rubbers on the other.

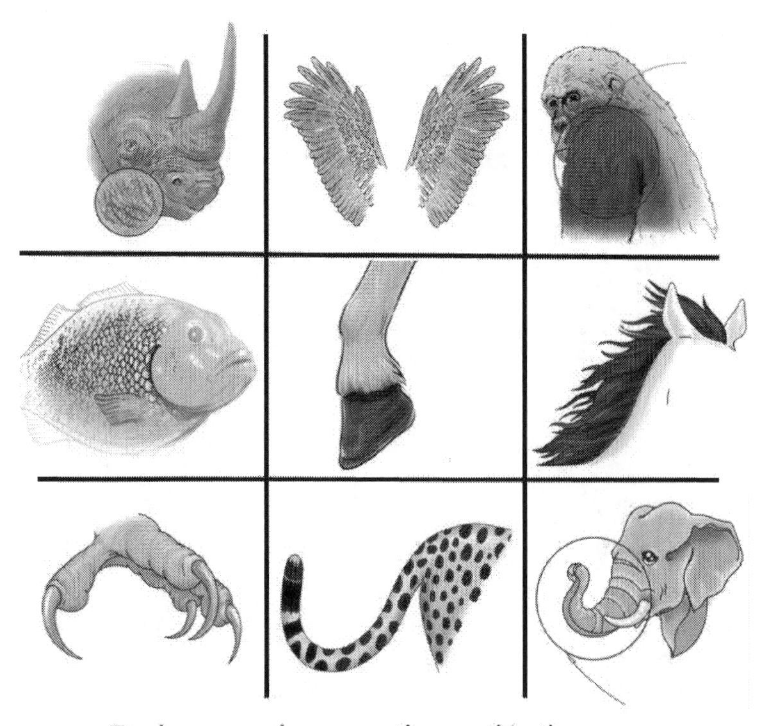

To place a marker name the word in the square. Flashcards from teachingenglishgames.com/esl-flashcards

do	you	it
he	she	does
they	we	I

To place a marker make a question using the word in the square.

cow	pig	cat
dog	lion	fish
bird	ant	duck

To place a marker translate the word into your own language.

The players first decide which marker they are using. One player starts by naming a picture and placing a marker on the picture. The second player now has a turn, naming one of the remaining available pictures and placing a marker on it. Continue until one of the players manages to form a line of three markers. Lines of three can be formed horizontally, vertically and diagonally.

Intermediate players can make sentences about the picture rather than just name the object represented. Players cannot place a marker unless they can name the picture in the square or make up a correct sentence with the word.

One Lemon

Category: Easy Speaking
Group size: Small group to a class of 30
Level: Beginner
Materials: None
Age: 4 to 12
Pace: Calm

I love the absurdity of this game. Use it for numbers as described below, or replace numbers with vocabulary words.

How to Play

Put the students in a circle or play at desks if there is no space. Each player has a number. The teacher goes into to the middle of the circle and says:

"One lemon
Half a lemon
Calls three lemons"

Immediately, student number three goes to the middle and says:

"Three lemons
Half a lemon
Calls ten lemons"

Students must be on alert when they are called. If they don't react immediately they lose their opportunity to go into the middle, or they are out and must sit down.

To use other vocabulary simply replace the word lemon with a different noun. Combine with adjectives to practise word order, for example:

"One brown eye
Half a brown eye
Calls three brown eyes".

After a few people have been in the middle switch to "blue nose" and the next student says:

"One blue nose
Half a blue nose
Calls eleven blue noses".

It doesn't make sense anyway so use it with whatever language you like. However make sure the phrases are correct and plurals are used properly. This is a drill so accuracy is important.

With more than 25 children put students in pairs so that there are two of each number. They can then come into the middle together and speak at the same time. This will allow more children to participate with less hanging around. Another way to involve everybody is to have the whole circle say the first two lines all together. Only the third line is said by the person in the middle alone.

One Up Stand Up

Category: Speaking
Group size: Small group to a class of 30
Level: Beginner to Intermediate
Materials: Picture flashcards
Age: 4 to 12
Pace: Wake up

Every player including you holds a picture. Students sit at their desks with eyes closed, heads in hands. Tap a student lightly on the shoulder saying, "One up, stand up!" He or she stands up. Show him a picture to name or make a sentence with according to the target language you are practising.

Now you and the student each tap a seated student on the shoulder and say, "Two up, stand up!" The two chosen students stand up and the exchange is repeated. Now there are four people standing. All four choose four seated students, tap them lightly and say, "Three up stand up". And so on until the whole class is standing. If you wish to repeat this, have all students swap pictures, sit down, heads in hands and start again.

If students are hesitant more preparation is needed with the target structure using a group speaking game such as True or False, or any of the step 3 games where children repeatedly ask the same questions in unison to drill them thoroughly before being expected to use the language alone.

Oranges

Category: Speaking – good end of term game
Group size: 6 to 40
Level: Beginner to Lower Intermediate
Materials: One orange or round object per team
Age: 4 to 12
Pace: Wake up to Excitable

Have teams form lines and give an orange to the first player in each line. On the command "ready, steady, go!" players race to pass the orange down to the end of the line, without touching it with their hands. The orange must be passed under the chin.

All players in class say a rhyme or sing a song together while passing the orange down and they must get the orange down to the end of the line before the end of the chant.

Alternatively have the person passing the orange say something to the one receiving it - use any language you would like to practise, from simple sentences such as greetings, phrases such as "Here you are!" to question and answers such as "Where are you from?" "I'm from London". Use any language. Passing the oranges is just fun packaging for it.

Pass the Box

Category: Speaking
Group size: 5 to 40
Level: Beginners to Intermediate
Materials: A box, or for larger groups several boxes, with a selection of items or pictures
Age: 4 to 12
Pace: Wake up

How to play

In this variation of Pass the Parcel there is no unwrapping, only a box with a lid that is passed round the class and which contains a mystery item. Pass round several boxes at once with a big group. Play music or have players sing a song or say a rhyme. Interrupt the music, song or rhyme unexpectedly.

The player(s) holding a box take the lid off and name the item, either a real item or a picture of one, although real items are better. They can also answer a question or make up a sentence about the item depending on the degree of difficulty relevant to your group. If the player cannot name the item in the box, or cannot answer the question about it, get help from the group, and then give that player a forfeit. See Forfeits for ideas.

After each box has been opened go round and replace the items without players seeing. Ask them to put their head in their hands while you do this. If you ask players to close their eyes they will all be squinting to see what you are doing! Or to save time if you have a large class, prior to the game give each player a picture card. When a student has had a turn opening the box he takes out the item and replaces it with his own picture card. Continue playing with the new objects or cards students have placed in the boxes.

More advanced language ideas

Aside from simple question and answer drills for beginners to lower intermediates, use the game for any questions such as:
What is it used for?
Is it something we need and why?
Would you want one? Why?

Materials

Garage sales or boot fairs are good places to pick up mini plastic animals, dolls' house furniture, and all sorts of small sized items. Failing having real items substitute picture cards or word flash cards.

Pass the Parcel

Category: Speaking – good end of term game
Group size: Small group activity
Level: Beginner to Intermediate
Materials: A present wrapped in many layers
Age: 4 to 10
Pace: Wake up

Materials

This game does take preparation with material you cannot use again so it is best suited to end of term or a small class. Wrap something up in many layers of paper, plastic bags, newspaper, different sized boxes, bubble wrap, material or anything else that comes to mind. An idea for an item to wrap is a large packet of dried fruits or a healthy snack that the parcel winner may share out with the whole class, in this way no one feels left out.

How to play

Sit your group in a circle and play some music. The players pass the package round the circle. Use more than one package for a big group. Every time the music stops the player holding a package unwraps one layer of the wrapping. The music and the game continue until finally the present is revealed, and the one who unwraps the last layer gets to keep the gift. If you do not have music get the group to sing a song, which you interrupt unexpectedly by clapping your hands or blowing a whistle. If you go to the end of the song every time it isn't quite so interesting and the children will try and hold on to the parcel until the song is over.

Make sure that everyone has a turn unwrapping a layer and you can rig this by clapping or stopping the music at the appropriate time. Younger children will not notice you rigging the game but the older ones will pick up on it and generally they don't like playing games that are rigged, as they don't see the point, so try to be subtle.

Tip: If the gift can be related to learning such as an English comic, or a sticker in English then so much the better.

Language ideas

Use any language with this game. Firstly there is a language speaking opportunity in singing a song as the parcel goes round, and secondly a question and answer may be included each time someone unwraps a layer. The group can ask a question in unison which those doing the unwrapping have to reply to. If you want to be really mean then those with a parcel must forfeit their turn if they cannot answer the question correctly. If you do this with a four year old they will probably burst into tears, so I only suggest this twist to the game if you are playing with older children.

Pass the Pictures

Category: Speaking
Group size: 5 to 40
Level: Beginner to Intermediate
Materials: Picture flash cards
Age: 4 to 12
Pace: Wake up

Have the class or group sit in a circle and pass a picture round, such as a picture of a nurse. Each player takes the picture and says, "He's a nurse" (if it is a male nurse of course). Leaving an interval of 5 players pass a second picture round, such as, "he's a diver". Each picture makes a complete circuit of the group with everyone saying the required sentence or word. If students do not know the word they ask someone next to them for help, but cannot pass the picture on until they have named it out loud. When you clap your hands, or blow a whistle everyone stops and those holding the picture are given a forfeit.

Classroom variant with children at desks

Hold up a picture and name it, then pass it to a child who names it and passes it on to any other child. Wait a few seconds and then pass out another picture, naming it. Give it to the same child as before or if you have a large class give it to a child somewhere else in the room. Keep handing out pictures until you have one picture to every three children. At various points during the game blow a whistle or give a signal and all those holding pictures do a forfeit. See under Forfeits for ideas.

Phonemes - thoughts on teaching the phonemic alphabet

Learning about phonemes is not essential in order to speak a language well. This is a fact as I learned several languages fluently with no conscious knowledge of individual phonemes. However I hasten to add that the languages I learned were all from the same Indo-European root and then Anglo-Saxon and Latin roots. There were therefore far fewer completely new sounds to grapple with.

Teaching phonemes can help enormously when learning a non-related language such as a Thai person learning English. Phonemes would be less essential with a German person learning English where many sounds are the same and there are relatively few totally new sounds. As well as making things easier for the student once the new phonemes are learned, this knowledge gives independence from the teacher in working out pronunciation.

How can you decide if you need to teach phonemes? I would say listen to the results you are achieving in class. If you clearly see there are pronunciation issues that lead to confusion in meaning then it is worth taking a step back to learn phonemes. I say take a step back because it can feel like that. However with this solid foundation in pronunciation your students will become better English speakers in the medium to long term.

Do not expect to see amazing results right away. You need to go over phonemes regularly, little and often. New neural pathways need to be built as students learn the facial position for each new sound, some of which will be utterly new to them and their muscles will need to integrate these new movements.

These games are excellent for phonemes and pronunciation in this book are: Chinese Whispers, Phonemes - Wall Charts, Phoneme Hangman, Phoneme Race, Pronunciation Game, Pronunciation Hands Up Game, Pronunciation: C for Consonant, V for Vowel. Any of the games in this book may be used for phonics, for example, Writing Race.

From a teacher: 'I liked the first Writing Race game you sent me and I used it for a phonics lesson with my grade ones. I made pictures with the sounds for each word on the flashcard. I divided the children into 3 groups of 9, with the children numbered from 1 to 9. I called the children using their numbers. Those called came to the front, looked at the pictures, and went back to their groups to spell the word or name of the picture. The children enjoyed this.'

Phoneme Hangman

Category: Saying sounds
Group size: 1 to 30
Level: Beginner to Intermediate
Materials: None
Age: 6 to Adult
Pace: Calm

See Hangman for the full game description. Use this game if you are teaching phonemes with phonemic script. This game allows students to say sounds and see what they look like in phonemic script. It helps young learners understand that phonemic script is made up of sounds and not letters. They also see an instant transcription of the sounds they make into the script.

Think of a word and the phonemic script for it such as the word wish. Write up __ __ __ on the board. The children guess which sounds are in the word by making a sound, which you then transcribe on the board as phonemic script. If the sound is in the word you fill in one of the blanks. If not you write that symbol on the board so students can see what it looks like. If students give you sounds that are already on the board point to the corresponding symbol. Students continue until the word is filled in.

Phoneme Race

Category: Recognising new phonemes and revising them
Group size: 2 to 40
Level: All levels to learn phonemes and improve pronunciation
Materials: Words on cards or the board

Age: 6 to 12
Pace: Wake up

Put 2 to 4 phoneme symbols on the board. If you are revising use a greater number. If you see children are struggling then play with fewer symbols. Write out about five words for each sound on cards or paper. Put students into small teams. A child from each team collects a word card from the teacher and returns to his or her group. Together the team decide by saying the word which phoneme it matches and a student writes this on the back of the card. Another student from the team returns to the teacher who checks the phoneme. If correct the team keep that card, the aim being to collect as many as possible during the game. The teacher then gives another card to the student and the game continues until the teacher has no more cards to give out.

To play this with no cards the teacher writes the words up on the board. The students decide in pairs or very small groups which phoneme matches the words on the board and in a limited time they match the words with the phonemes either by coming up to the board and writing the words out under the correct phoneme or by making a chart at their desks. Allow less time than is needed to complete the task to keep the children alert and thinking on their feet.

Now ask teams to race each other to find another word that also has that phoneme.

Phonemes Wall Charts

Category: Recognising phonemes
Group size: 2 to 35
Level: All levels to learn phonemes and improve pronunciation
Materials: Large pieces of coloured paper, or plain paper and coloured pens
Age: 6 to 12
Pace: Wake up

This is an ongoing activity that can be done over a term while introducing and learning phonemes. It is well worth learning phonemes to give your students a tool that will allow them to develop good pronunciation. For each phoneme you introduce use a matching picture such as a picture of cheese for the long /i:/ sound. After some initial drilling using a step 1 listening game like Jump the Line, stick up a large piece of paper on the wall with the phoneme and the picture at the top and the word 'cheese' written underneath. In the first lesson start with two of these pieces of paper on the wall and add to them over the coming lessons until you have all the 42 phonemes up, or all the most relevant phonemes for your English language learners.

Next play Show Me where you call out a phoneme and the children point to the correct wall chart. In the same lesson and in subsequent lessons give out words on cards and give the students a time limit to stick their word or words on or under the correct chart. Use pictures or words for this. For example a child with a picture of some feet will stick the picture or word card on the "cheese" wall chart.

With a large class use repeat wall charts on each side of the class so the children do not all converge on the same chart. This is less of a problem when you have many different sounds up, but when you only have a handful of sounds duplicate them to keep the children spread out.

This activity can be carried out in silence if you have any kind of discipline problems but it is best if the children say their phoneme or word as they are searching for the matching wall chart. I don't recommend playing music during this game since it focuses on sounds and the music might conflict and be too distracting. Then send the children round again to try and spot any errors on the charts. While the children are doing this the teacher also checks them.

Pictionary

Category: Speaking
Group size: 2 to 40

Level: Beginner to Intermediate
Materials: Paper and pens or class board
Age: 5 to 12
Pace: Wake up

This is the classic Pictionary game where one player draws an object and the other players try to be the first to guess what it is. This game works well in teams of 6 players or so. It may be that you need to stop the game before everyone has had a go at drawing. Remember to always stop the games while the players are enjoying them, before they show signs of boredom.

Each team member takes a turn to draw an object specified by you. Run each picture as a separate race, but with a big class it is recommended to run it as a relay race straight through from start to finish. One member from each team comes up to you and you whisper the item in his or her ear, or you show the written word, or a picture of the item. They then race back to their group and draw the item. Their team must name the item in English.

When it has been correctly named the next team member goes up to find out what he or she is to draw, and so on until all five or six rounds have been played. The winning team is the one that finishes first.

Picture Flashcards

Category: Speaking
Group size: 1 to a large class
Level: Beginner to Intermediate
Materials: Picture flash cards
Age: 4 to 12
Pace: Calm to Wake up

For lightning speed vocabulary revision hold up pictures and have players call out the name of the item. Divide the class into teams and give each team one minute to name as many pictures as possible while you show them flashcards rapidly. Ideally have a pupil on a stopwatch to keep it fair and another pupil counting up the words the teams name correctly.

Hundreds of downloadable flashcards are available from the author's website, please see below in the resources section for details.

Large class variant

Divide your class into teams and hold up 5 different pictures per team. The team must name as many as possible and score a point for each picture named. Move on to the next team with different pictures, or a mix of some of the same and some new ones.

To prevent the same person naming all the pictures, have a rule where a person can only name one picture and then must allow other team members to answer. Put the best students at the board scoring for their team.

To make the game exciting show each picture for a maximum of 3 seconds and go through the flashcards quicker if the children can keep up. In this way you move around your teams quickly.

Piggy in the Middle

Category: Speaking
Group size: 4 to a small class
Level: Beginner to Intermediate
Materials: None
Age: 4 to 8
Pace: Wake up

As the pace of this game is sedate play around the desks. Otherwise form a circle with one student in the middle, eyes blindfolded. The other players walk round the circle chanting a rhyme, singing a song, or asking a question in unison. At the end of the rhyme, song or question, all players stop, the piggy in the middle spins round and points at someone. Where a question was used the piggy will answer it while pointing. The person being pointed to is next to go in the middle. The new piggy takes his or her place in the middle of the circle and the chant, song or question is repeated, and so on. Here are some examples of rhymes:

"Mirror, mirror on the wall, who is the fairest of them all?" Piggy in the middle spins round points at someone and says, "You are!"

"This little piggy went to market,
This little piggy stayed at home,
This little piggy had roast beef,
This little piggy had none,
And this little piggy went wee wee wee wee all the way home!"

On the "wee wee wee wee" piggy in the middle spins round and points at someone on "home!"

Piggy in the Middle Guessing Variant

Category: Speaking
Group size: Small group activity
Level: Beginner to Intermediate
Materials: None
Age: 4 to 8
Pace: Wake up

How to play

Here is an example of how to play this game using vocabulary for professions: Form a circle with a pupil in the middle. Show the 'piggy' a picture flashcard, such as 'doctor' and then blindfold the 'piggy'. Hand out a few doctor pictures randomly around the group - say one picture to every three people in the circle. The children in the circle then say their rhyme, which can be anything you like, such as:

What does he do? Do be do do,
Do be do do, What does he do?
OR

What does he do? Buzz, buzz, buzz.
I want to know what he does.

Piggy spins round and points at someone saying, "He's a doctor". If Piggy points at someone who has a picture, then Piggy gets to keep that picture, or is awarded a point, or is allowed another go in the middle. If Piggy points at someone who does not have a picture then he re-joins the circle, and someone else is Piggy.

Ping Pang Pong

Category: Speaking
Group size: Up to a class of about 30 for best results
Level: Beginner to Intermediate
Materials: None
Age: from 6 to adult
Pace: Calm

A teacher called Alka sent me this game. Divide your class into groups of three students. Number the class from one to thirty, or however many students you have. The teacher starts by saying; "ping, pang, pong number 2. This means the members of that group are up. Number 1 says ping, number 2 says pang and number three says pong, followed by a new number, such as 10. Now the members of a new group are up. Number 10 says ping, number 11 says pang and number 12 says pong, plus a new number.

If any team says a number from its own team it is out, OR if a player says the number of any team that is already out, again the team is out. Finally, if a team mixes up the ping pang pong order the whole team is out.

A slightly simpler way to play is to dispense with the teams. As before give each student a number. Now start by saying ping pang pong number 3. Student number 3 says ping, number 4 says pang and number 5 says pong, PLUS a random number. The game continues for as long as you like, or until there are only five people left playing, who become the winners.

Use this game for speaking practice with any vocabulary. Simply replace ping pang pong with three words, such as cow pig duck, number 7.

Ping Pong

Category: Reading, writing and speaking
Group size: 2 to a large class
Level: Beginner to Intermediate
Materials: Paper and pens or class board
Age: 6 to adult
Pace: Calm

This is an excellent vocabulary revision game and drill for short phrases. Players form teams. Give a time limit for teams to write down as many words as possible in a given theme. When the time is up teams take it in turns to call out one word. The opposite team must hit back with a different word until the teams run out of new words. The winning team is the one that speaks last.

As with most of the games, this one is very adaptable. It is up to you to make the language and vocabulary as hard or as easy as you like. Use categories of words such as sports or food, or play with short sentences like, "I'm French, I'm Spanish, I'm English" and so on.

Large class variant

Divide your class in teams and have the whole class stand up. Name a theme such as transport - children call out words in that theme - restricted to one word per child. Once a child has given a word he or she sits down. A word can only be used once. The winning team is the one with everyone sitting down first. At that point start a new round or move on to another game.

You may need to go through several themes before a whole team is seated depending on the extent of your pupils' vocabulary. Seated students are allowed to whisper words to those standing.

That prevents a slow student from being left standing and feeling stupid and it also encourages team spirit.

Use simple vocabulary revision for this game, or have the pupils call out a sentence, which includes a word from the theme and your desired target structure. Drill the target structure with some step three speaking games beforehand so this game flows well.

Potato Race

Category: Speaking
Group size: 2 to a small class
Level: Beginner to Intermediate
Materials: Potatoes and spoons
Age: 4 to 12
Pace: Wake up to Excitable

This game is an excuse to ask and answer questions while racing with a potato balanced on a spoon. Below is an example of how this game can be played with a class divided into teams of 6, however adapt it to your needs. P stands for player. There are two spoons and potatoes per team.

How to play

P1 runs to P4, carrying a potato on a spoon without dropping it, and asks P4 a question, which P4 answers. Simultaneously P5 runs to P2, carrying a potato and exchanging a question and answer. When P4 has taken the potato from P1 he or she runs to P3. Meanwhile P2 runs to P6. Finally P6 runs to P5 and P3 runs to P1. Everyone has had a turn.

With 4 year olds you might want to reduce the distance travel with their potatoes. You could introduce penalties if a player drops a potato, such as starting at the beginning again, or naming four vocabulary words on the spot before continuing. It is possible to play this game in the aisles of the classroom.

Language ideas

Use any question and answer vocabulary ranging from the simple "What's your name?" to the complex. This is a drill game so accuracy is important.

Preposition Challenge

Category: speaking
Group size: any – pair work
Level: Beginner
Materials: Pictures or scenes
Age: 6 to adult
Pace: Calm

How to play

Children work in pairs. Child A holds up a picture of for example a cat under a chair for ten seconds while child B studies it. Child A then places the picture face down and asks a question such as, "Where is the cat?" or, "Is the cat on or under the chair?" If child B answers correctly that's a point. Child A asks the next question, such as "What colour is the chair?" until child B cannot answer. At that point child A holds up the picture for another 10 seconds before continuing through the questions. Child A holds the picture up three times, and child B tries to answer as many correct questions as possible. The point scoring is of course optional though it does give an incentive to concentrate.

For this game you need pictures of scenes such as a room with people in it, places or views. Try a furniture catalogue with pictures of rooms. Use scenes from the class textbook if you use one. Stick cute pictures onto that of cartoon characters, or animals. Other sources for good pictures might be holiday brochures, or a movie poster. The web will provide where all else fails.

With your demo picture prepared play this with the class, holding up your picture and asking questions. Let the children see the fun collage that you made and have them each make one for homework. Use these in the next class. Scan or photocopy the good ones and use them again in future as revision or with new classes.

Preposition Mimes

Category: acting out and naming prepositions
Group size: 2 to 40
Level: Beginner
Materials: None
Age: 5 to 12
Pace: Calm

A simple game to practise prepositions creatively. This can be done with one student but it is more fun when pupils work in small groups. Give each pair or group a word card with a preposition on it for them to demonstrate. Each group illustrates their preposition using their bodies and holds the position. Then let a few students go around the room and call out the words being demonstrated. Once a preposition has been correctly named the group demonstrating it sits down again. Repeat but swap in the students who named the formations.

The class will enjoy making physical representations of the prepositions and will be far more likely to remember them. For example "under" could be one student lying down while the others make a bridge over him or her by getting down on all fours - legs on one side of the student on the floor, hands on the other, or they could hold their arms over the student if your floor is too dirty. As always perform a demonstration of the concept with a few students in front of the class before starting.

Add zest to the game by bringing two groups to the front. Give them a word to do simultaneously and let them race to demonstrate the preposition while the class guess. A less competitive angle but still exciting would be to let the class start forming their shape but at any moment you call out "Freeze!" At that point everyone must freeze and then see whether students can guess the shapes. Dish out points for successful shapes if this motivates your class.

Pronunciation Chart Game

Category: Speaking and thinking about pronunciation
Group size: 2 to 40 and possibly more
Level: Beginner to Advanced
Materials: Word cards
Age: 5 to adult
Pace: Calm

This is a version of the Phonemes Wall Chart Game where students stick their word cards on the board or on the wall according to the sound.

How to play

This example uses past simple verb ending pronunciation. Draw three empty columns on the board with a header for each column, /t/, /d/ and /Id/. Make an entry into each column by way of example. Column one, talked, column two, burned and column three wanted. Demonstrate the three ways of saying the 'ed' verb ending to be sure students can tell the difference.

Display a selection of past simple verbs on the board. These can be on cards or written at the edge of the board. The students' task is to copy the columns and write each word in the correct column to match the pronunciation of the verb ending. Students do this by saying the words, not only reading them. Simultaneously students should take turns to come to the board and move the word cards into the correct columns either by moving the cards physically or rubbing out the verb from the teacher's list and re-writing it in the correct column on the board.

Periodically during the activity the teacher can stop students and say that there are a certain number of verbs placed or written incorrectly on the board. The teacher will not say which verbs are incorrect, only how many are wrongly placed - the students have to figure it out and make the adjustment themselves. Make sure the students at the board rotate often.

Rather than give out the rule for this let the students try to match their verbs to the correct column by saying the words repeatedly and choosing the pronunciation that seems easiest to them. Moving the cards into the columns is good for tactile learners. Examples of words are:

/t/ liked, talked, danced, looked, dressed, watched, hoped, helped, finished, missed, kissed, washed, locked and worked

/d/ learned, played, tried, cried, lived, sewed, showed, ordered, happened, rained, payed, prayed, enjoyed, screamed and opened

/Id/ wanted, floated, hated, needed, waited, visited, painted and intended

The above example is for the past simple verb 'ed' endings however this idea works with any vocabulary where you match the word to the phoneme or sound on the board. Some matching sounds are light, bright, site and bite or the words hair, bear, care, share, dare, pear and chair.

Pronunciation Feather Game

Category: Speaking - correct pronunciation for b versus p, and h.

Group size: 2 to 40

Level: Beginner to Advanced

Materials: Something fluffy that moves when you blow on it
Age: 5 to adult
Pace: Calm

This exercise is humorously demonstrated in the film My Fair Lady during an elocution lesson.

Children work in pairs and each pair has a feather or fluffy object that moves when you blow on it. I use pens that have fake feathers on the end, as these are readily available in my local toy store. This game works beautifully with a candle flame too but that is only suitable in a one on one situation where you keep an eye on the candle.

You will notice that if you place a fluffy object in front of your mouth and say, "bat" the fluff will not move much but if you say "pat" it is as if a gale force wind hit the fluff. The same is true to a lesser degree with "high, hate and hello" as opposed to "I, ate and yellow". Children take it in turns to say words on a list you provide and give each other points for making the fluff move or not according to the word.

Pronunciation Game

Category: Speaking - correct pronunciation
Group size: 2 to 40
Level: Beginner to Advanced
Materials: None
Age: 5 to adult
Pace: Calm

Put the students in pairs, threes or fours. Spell out or write a word that is frequently mispronounced. With younger children who are not reading or writing yet show a picture card. The children confer with each other as to exactly how this word is pronounced. A spokesperson from each pair or group says the word out loud and the teacher tells the pair to write down a one or a two. When all the pairs have given their version the teacher pronounces it correctly and says that all the number twos have a point. In each round the children never know whether the one or the two is correct and that prevents them from just copying each other. You'll find that the children take great care when points are at stake!

Play again with a different word and this time a different team starts first and all spokespeople rotate. Play with up to ten words.

Pronunciation Hands Up

Category: Listening for phonemes and pronunciation
Group size: 2 to any class size
Level: All levels for pronunciation
Materials: None
Age: 4 to adult
Pace: Calm

This listening game works with phonemes or pronunciation of words. The teacher repeats a word several times and then unexpectedly changes to another word using a different phoneme. Pick words that your students have difficulty with. For example a Spanish student would be likely to have trouble differentiating between ship and sheep. A French student will probably have trouble with worth and worse or earth and hearse. Japanese students will have a job with the letter r and so on.

The teacher says "lorry, lorry, lorry, lorry, lolly, lolly, lolly, lolly, lorry, lorry, lorry." When the students hear the change they raise their hands. When the change reverts back to lorry students lower their hands.

With a small group do this in pairs and award points to the first student to put his hand up. Deduct points for hands going up before the change! With a bigger class split students into teams. Count the number of times you say "lolly" before all students on that team have their hands up. Repeat with Team 2 and award the point to the team that was fastest.

A big challenge is to let the students take over from you with the speaking. That certainly makes students focus on how they pronounce words.

Pronunciation Pictures

Category: Speaking
Group size: 2 to 40
Level: Beginner to Intermediate
Materials: Pens and paper for the children
Age: 4 to 12
Pace: Calm

Put a selection of words or pictures on the board in contrasting pairs or groups that you know your class have trouble with. Then in pairs let one child tell the other what to draw from those on the board. The children will understand how important good pronunciation is when they see if their partner draws what they said rather than something different. For example a Japanese student may have difficulty saying lorry and lolly, so these would be two words or pictures to put up on the board.

If you write a selection of totally unrelated sounds the activity will not work on good pronunciation. The idea is to put up very similar sounding words so that children have to concentrate on saying them correctly so that their partner draws the correct item.

This can be a one-off activity or an ongoing one. These pictures can go on the walls and the children can add to them any time they think of another matching word. As a continuation of the pair work above, help the children by having picture flashcards of vocabulary up on the board for them to consider and choose from to add to the wall charts. Without this most likely the younger children and early beginners will not be able to come up with any words on their own.

Pronunciation Word Stress

Category: Listening
Group size: Any
Level: Beginner to Advanced
Materials: None, or optional fly swatters
Age: 6 upwards

Pace: Calm

Write a list words on the board as shown below. Each word is repeated for as many times as it has syllables. Underline a different syllable with each word. The underline represents where the stress falls and only one is correct. For example:

Television Television Television Television
Happily Happily Happily
Unbelievable Unbelievable Unbelievable Unbelievable
Unbelievable

Divide your class into four teams and give each a number. Call out the word, with the correct stress and say, "number twos". The number twos race up to the board, grab the optional fly swatters and swat the correct word from the four you have on the board. If you have mixed abilities then let your better students have the task of saying the words for the others. With some longer words there may well be stress in two places

This is a listening game so it can in theory be played in silence. Any noise and bang! Deduct a point from the noisy team.

Proverb Pairs

Category: Writing and Speaking
Group size: Any
Level: Beginner to Advanced
Materials: Proverbs
Age: 6 upwards
Pace: Calm

To save photocopies write proverbs on the board in two columns as far away from each other on the board as possible, and not in the same order. One half of the proverb is in column A and the other half in column B. Mix up where you write the first part of the proverb so that column A does not only have the beginnings of proverbs.

Pupils pair up and copy either column A or column B. Once pupils have copied their column of partial proverbs, hide or clear the board. Players cannot show their papers to each other. Player A reads out one half of a proverb and player B looks for and reads out the second half. The players must match up all their proverbs through speaking alone.

Use poetry, riddles and metaphors for advanced students. With beginners use basic sentences from the curriculum.

GAMES Q-R

Question and Answer

Category: Speaking
Group size: All class sizes divided into teams
Level: Beginner to Intermediate
Materials: None
Age: 4 to 12
Pace: Wake up

Version using a ball for small groups

One player with the ball throws it and asks a question. The player who catches the ball answers the question and throws the ball to someone else. This person catches the ball, asks a question and so on. If you just want the class to practise the answer then you throw the ball and ask the question, for example, "What's 10 minus 3?" Throw the ball to someone. They catch it and answer "7" and throw the ball back to you. You then ask another question to someone else.

If the four year olds cannot catch the ball they can roll it along the ground to each other.

Version with no ball for larger groups

Ask the class a series of questions to reinforce the question structure you are teaching. For example: "Do you like apples?" The class respond out loud and all together with either "Yes I do", or "No I don't", according to their personal preference. If their answer is "Yes I do", they stand up, and if it is "No I don't", they sit down. If they are already sitting down and their next answer is still no, they answer "No I don't" and remain seated. Likewise they remain standing if their answer is "Yes I do".

This game has the benefit of having the class hear the sentence structure repeatedly, practise the answer, revise vocabulary and be actively engaged through movement while remaining calm and disciplined.

Large class variant

With your students in teams, tell everyone to write out a question using your target structure or tense. Randomly select one student from each team and ask to hear the question, with the proviso that the student says his question out loud from memory rather than reading it out. If the question is correct, that team scores a point. Now ask the class to write out an answer and repeat as above asking for an answer from a different student.

Although students do not all speak everyone has to work hard because no one knows who will be picked to read out the sentence or question. If a student does not have a question ready that team forfeit the chance to earn a point.

Continue until you feel the question and answer target structures are well ingrained - but do not play for more than ten minutes at most. If students need more work switch to a different game but continue with the same language.

For intermediates allow your pupils to come up with the actual question form by telling them to ask for the time or find out someone's age and so on.

Question and Answer Lottery Match

Category: Writing and speaking
Group size: All group sizes including large classes
Level: Beginner to Advanced
Materials: Questions
Age: 6 to 12
Pace: Wake up

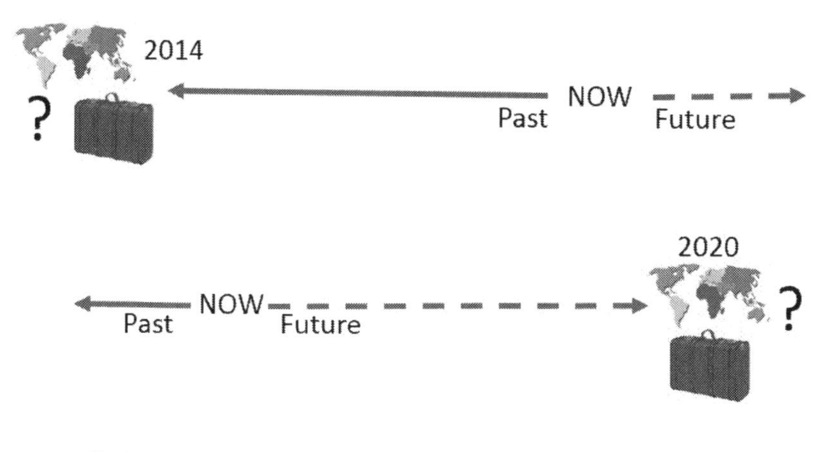

Set up

Before you play ask your class to call out different questions to refresh their memories. If necessary draw prompts on the board to elicit these questions such as a clock face for "What time is it?" or a person with a timeline graphic for "Where are you going?" Time lines are not infallible, especially if your students are Japanese and read things backwards in comparison to you, therefore be sure to explain them. For example the graphics below could be depictions of "Where did you go in 2007?" and "Where are you going in 2020?"

If you are stuck for drawing prompts put up the question words on the board such as what, when, where, how and who, brainstorm and leave those as prompts.

How to play

Divide your class into teams and ask half of the teams to write any type of question while the other half write any type of answer. Alternatively each pupil writes out a question and an answer to another question. For example "What time is it?" and "I'm going to London". A student from Team 1 asks a question, preferably from memory. If the question is correct that team scores a point. If incorrect someone with a question from another team has a chance. Once you have a correct question, the others race to stand up and give a matching answer. If the answer is correct it wins a point for that team.

For example a member of team 1 stands up and asks "How old are you?" You say "Correct." Now any class member from any other team who has a matching answer such as "I'm 7" can stand up and call out the answer. If correct they earn a point for their team. Now ask a member of team 2 for their question, and so on.

Pupils must have the answer on their paper to call it out. That is why it is a form of lottery, and not just a test to see whether they can answer the question.

Quiz Race

Category: Reading with more advanced writing variant
Group size: Variants for small and large classes
Level: Beginner to Advanced
Materials: Questions
Age: 6 to 12
Pace: Wake up

Easy variant for all group sizes

Write out a list of questions. Give them out to your class with a time limit to answer them all. An easy idea is to start in the classroom with questions such as:

"How many chairs/windows/doors/children/desks are there in the classroom?"

"How many doors/teachers/gardens/windows/children are there in the school?" The children with the closest answer win.

More advanced idea for smaller groups

Divide the class into groups and tell them to prepare a quiz. Each team chooses its own topic, such as a favourite band or cartoon character. Each team member comes up with one or two questions about that topic. The child writing the question must know the answer to it. Allow 5 minutes or so for the children to write their questions. If necessary put some question types on the board to help out. Put the teams into panels, take all the questions in and have a TV type quiz to see which team wins.

Rapid Grab It

Category: Listening
Group size: 2 to 20
Level: Beginner to Lower Intermediate
Materials: Real objects
Age: 4 to 12
Pace: Wake up

How to play

This game is similar to Rapid Reaction in that it is a race to pick out an item. Have a pile of objects such as plastic animals or laminated letters and divide each group into pairs or threes. For example with a group of 12 players you would have three number 1s, three number 2s, three number 3s and three number 4s. Say a sentence of your choosing, such as "Number 1, Out in the big wide jungle I saw a lion!" The three number 1s race to pick out the plastic lion.

Four to five year olds

If you have four to five year olds you really want to have a lion for each of them to pick out, or ask them to pick something out in turn. In any event make sure that everyone gets something during the course of the game.

Materials

Items you could use include coloured pens to do colours, plastic or real fruit and vegetables, doll's house furniture, Barbie dolls (pick out the Barbie with the pink skirt and blue top), classroom items, household items, different coloured numbers or letters. If laminated vocabulary flashcards will last but if you do not have any the class can make these in a few minutes on paper, play with those and throw them away at the end as they will probably be crumpled and torn by the end of the game.

Large class variant with children out of their seats and moving around. Another way to play is to scatter objects about the class on tables and ask, "Who can find such and such an object?" E.g. spread out coloured numbers or letters and ask, "Who can find a yellow six?"

Rapid Reaction

Category: Listening

Group size: 2 to 16. If possible have two groups of 8 rather than one bigger group.

Level: Beginner to Intermediate

Materials: One set of pictures for every 8 players, Fly swatters if possible

Age: 4 to 12

Pace: Wake up

Use this game to introduce new grammar or revise a tricky structure that students have not fully grasped. Do this by repeating sentences, which include one of the words on the board. This allows students to hear a new or difficult structure repeatedly while they are concentrating on listening out for a word that matches one on the board. Use picture cards for newly introduced vocabulary or for revision. Use word cards to revise spelling.

Lay out a number of picture cards with the group seated around. With 16 students lay out two sets of picture cards, with one set at one end of the group. Call out one of the pictures and the players race to touch it first. Rather than keeping score it is better to keep up a fast pace saying the words rapidly one after the other. This keeps the players on their toes and they have no time to mess around.

If the same students keep winning, give them the task of calling out the words instead of the teacher. Or you could get them to play with one hand behind their back. Normally it is the fastest player who touches the correct picture who wins, however allow the fastest two or three players on any given picture if you wish.

With young players aged 4 start by laying out two cards and then gradually add to them. With the young ones allow everyone to touch the card rather than laying emphasis on someone getting their first.

It is the way you say the words that makes this game lively or not. For example switch back and forth between two cards repeatedly and then suddenly say a different card. You will be sure to catch some of the children out. If the pace is too slow then this game is too easy and becomes boring.

Variant with fly swatters using the board

Draw or stick up pictures all over the board. Divide the class into two teams and place two or three students on chairs in front of the board, each holding a fly swatter. If a fly swatter is not readily available then improvise. A piece of card works although it is not as satisfying! As a variant you could try elastic bands, which children aim at the word on the board but this can lead to being silly.

Call out a word and the children race to swat it. Students at the board are allowed one swat only. The fastest student who is correct earns a point for his or her team, though using competition is optional, with this or any game. Any talking or messing around in the ranks, deduct points from the relevant team. Aside from the teacher saying the words this game should be played in total silence and if anyone else speaks the offending student immediately loses a point for his or her team. A strategy like this is essential to keep the class from becoming too excited.

Idea for bigger groups

To work around waiting too long, which leads to restlessness and boredom in class, give half the class a writing task while you play the game with the others and then swap around. To motivate the students writing to finish this task can be set for homework if not completed in class. If you take in this writing task and mark it students will take it more seriously. If some students are distracted into watching the game rather than completing their writing task, it is not that drastic since they will be learning by listening to the English used for the game.

Language ideas

Name the vocabulary word or give a clue about it such as "you use it to play tennis".

For speaking work players can ask you a question in unison such as "What do you do?" to which you reply "I'm a...Dentist!" The players then race to slap their hand or fly swatter down on the picture of the dentist.

Make this question as complex as you like, for example the players ask, "If you won the lottery, what would you buy?" You reply, "I would buy...a house!"

Reading Comprehension – A different challenge

Category: Reading
Group size: any
Level: Beginner to Advanced
Materials: Reading passages
Age: From 6 to adult
Pace: Calm

Reading Comprehension is something many of us are familiar with from our own school days. Generally students read a passage and then answer some mind bogglingly dull questions on the content. Here is a way to involve students while giving them more of a reason to pay attention to the content.

How to play

Give students a time limit to read a passage. Students now close books and write one to five questions about the text for their colleagues. One question would be easy to think of, five would be relatively difficult so adjust according to the level and age of your pupils.

Now students swap their questions with a neighbour. Give a time limit for everyone to answer these WITHOUT looking at the text again. Students swap back so the neighbour can mark the answers and give a score. Repeat the exercise with the same reading text, this time students write a different question/set of questions. Repeat and compare scores – normally the scores should be far higher the second time around.

The use of a time limit adds zest to the activity. Creating questions for colleagues involves students more in the task. Using memory alone to answer questions adds to the challenge and fun. It's not just a question of looking through the text but trying to remember it.

Alternative version: A simpler variant of the above idea is to again give a time limit to the class to look at a text. Students turn the text face down and get ready to answer your questions. You ask and students who know the answer jump up into the aisle and call out the answer. If correct that's a point for the team, if wrong then ALL the team points are eliminated!! This discourages students from jumping in before they are really sure what the answer is.

Inevitably with a game like this you'll have the brightest students doing all the work. Get around this by putting them all in one team together and let each team take a turn to answer. Even better is to bring up the brightest ones and let them run the quiz, making up and asking the questions, and keeping score on the board.

Reading Puzzle

Category: Reading
Group size: Any
Level: Beginner to Advanced
Materials: Text passages or dialogues
Age: From 6 up to adult
Pace: Calm

Give out sections of text chopped in half. For more advanced levels these could be anything from a sentence to whole paragraphs. Just as in Find Your Friend students mingle, reading each other's text and seeing if together they make a match.

To extend this activity and make it more challenging give each member of the class a sentence or short paragraph from a long story. Let the class have the joint target of constructing the whole story by sticking it together on a wall of the classroom, or working all around the class on four walls to let students be better spaced out. Stories with dialogues are useful and can be fun to piece together.

One could use four stories simultaneously, one wall of the classroom per story. The class do not know which story they have and start completely from scratch. When a child has placed his or her sentence he/she continues to participate by reading the pieces already up around the class and checking they make sense and moving anything that seems wrong.

Though the children are out of their seats this game should be played in total silence and anyone talking can be eliminated if necessary.

As a follow-up to this game use the wall texts for a treasure hunt. Call out a part of speech, a vocabulary word, any word starting with T or a character and let the children run to the walls and find an example.

Recognising Tenses

Category: Listening
Group size: Small group to a class
Level: Beginner to Intermediate
Materials: None
Age: 4 to 12
Pace: Wake up

This game is good to review several tenses and also to review two tenses while introducing one new one.

Small group version

Children stand in a circle. When you say a sentence in the present tense everyone moves one place to the left. When you say a sentence in the past tense everyone moves one place to the right and when you say a sentence in the future everyone scrambles to change places.

This can be varied as much as you like. Play with any mixture of tenses and add in extra movements such as clapping when hearing the present continuous and so on. If the scramble movement is too rowdy replace it with giving a high-five to a student next door.

Class version

This works in the same way as the small group version except that students remain seated at desks, or standing in the aisles. Instead of swapping places students do high-fives to the left, to the right and jump on the spot for future. Use any actions that work for you.

Relay Race

Category: Speaking

Group size: All class sizes with alternative version for very small groups

Level: Beginner to Advanced

Materials: Pictures are a good idea

Age: 4 to 12

Pace: Wake up

How to play

Put your group or class into teams of approximately 5 players per line. The one at the front has a picture of, say, a pizza. On your signal the first player in each line says to number 2 in the line: "Would you like some pizza?" Number 2 says "Yes please", takes the picture, turns to number 3 in the line and asks "Would you like some pizza?" number 3 says "Yes please", takes the pizza, turns to number 4, and so on until you reach the end of the line. The idea is to get the pizza down to the end of the line as quickly as possible. If you have a longer line of ten people for example, then you should pass down at least two different pictures, one after the other, to keep everyone involved.

Once all the pictures are at the bottom of the line the person at the end of the line runs up to the front of the class with them.

It is most important that the words are properly pronounced and that accuracy is not abandoned for speed. To ensure this name the first person in the line as a referee for that team. This referee must belong to another team so that he or she will referee properly. Swap the referees around, but make sure your better students have the task.

Language ideas

Use any language for this game, from simply naming the item and passing it down, to sentences with a particular verb tense or structure. Ideas are:

I am Shelley, you are Jane. Jane continues with I am Jane you are Michael, etc.

I am Shelley, she is Jane. Jane: I am Jane, he is Michael, etc.

Shelley: I love ice cream. Jane: I love chocolate.

Shelley: I love ice cream. Jane: she loves ice cream, I love chocolate. Michael: she loves chocolate, I love ice cream, etc.

Shelley: I like ice cream. What do you like? Jane: I like chocolate. What do you like? Michael: I like cake, etc.

Instead of a picture pass a message down the line, although it's not a bad idea to pass something physical, especially for children as it makes it more fun for them as they see the progress the message is making in tangible form. If this game does not work you probably need to either simplify the language to get the basics down or drill more with another game first.

Very small group version

Here's a way to use relay race with only 5 children - let them pass the language down the line once and time them with a stop watch. Then let them do it again and see if they can beat their time. Or instead of a stopwatch walk across the room from one wall to the other and they have to finish before you get to the other side. The first time saunter over there, and gradually speed up, but always let them finish before you!

Relay Race advanced variant

This game is useful for advanced and older students too if you would like to drill an aspect of language where there are frequent errors. Instead of handing down vocabulary cards or having set sentences repeated down the line of students give your pupils the more challenging task of coming up with their own sentences during the race. For example hand a picture or word card to the first student in each team and this student makes up a sentence with the word in it. The student then passes the card to the next person in the team and this person has to make up a different sentence. This allows intermediate students to work on speaking skills using a much wider range of language.

If you use this as a fluency game then you would not focus on correcting the language at all during the game. You might note a few errors and go over them on the board afterwards. Another way to play is to insist that the sentences be correct in order for the card to be passed. In this case you want the team to collaborate to correct any sentences with errors. You listen in and if you spot any errors as the cards are being passed you signal to the team and the students know they must work together to correct the error in order to pass the card on.

You cannot be a control freak with this game. It will be impossible to hear everything that is going on. Basically if you are doing an accuracy drill keep it sufficiently simple so that it is well within the students' grasp. If you are doing a fluency activity errors are inevitable and are to be accepted.

Remember and Write

Category: Writing
Group size: 2 to a large class
Level: Beginner to Advanced
Materials: Pictures or real objects
Age: 6 to 12
Pace: Calm

Display at least 12 pictures or objects at some place in the class where everyone can see them. Give the class a limited time to look at and memorise all the items. Then cover them over and allow a couple of minutes for everyone to write down as many items as they remember. Play with a list of words on the board to help pupils learn and remember spelling.

To practise a target structure with this vocabulary revision game then ask the pupils to write out a set sentence containing each of the words.

Rhyming Ping-Pong

Category: Reading, writing, speaking
Group size: 2 to a class
Level: Intermediate to Advanced
Materials: Pen and paper or the class board
Age: 8 to Adult
Pace: Calm

Have players get together in teams and write down all the words they can think of that have a certain spelling, or rhyme with each other. For example you could tell them to write down all the words that rhyme with the sound "A" as in LAY.

Intermediates might come up with words such as: lay, day, say, play, clay, pay, tray, bay, Fay, gay, hay, May, way, pray.

Advanced players might also come up with words such as: weigh, daily, neigh, neighbourly, fray, playful, delay, jay, nay, flay.

Give the teams a minute or two to write down their words. Then have a play-off where each team takes it in turns to call out one of their words. If a word has already been said it cannot be used again, and it must be crossed off the list.

When a team has no more words it is out and the remaining teams keep batting words backwards and forwards between themselves, until only one team is left.

The play off must be fast paced with a 4 second time frame for a team to return a word or the team is out. Adapt the number of seconds, but keep an eye on the pace of the game - the sense of urgency is what makes it fun.

Run and Write

Category: Listening, reading, writing and spelling
Group size: Up to 30 divided into groups of 3 to 4 or pairs
Level: Beginner to Intermediate
Materials: Lists of vocabulary or sentences, one set for each group.

Age: 6 to 12
Pace: Wake up

Give out a list of words to each group. Call out one of the words several times. Students hunt for that word in the list and as soon as they find it a leader from the group goes up to the board and writes that word from memory. When the leader has written the word correctly on the board he or she gives the teacher a high five. The first leader to give the teacher a high-five gets the point for that round. The role of leader is to rotate around the group, three words each.

Use sentences too. Students hunt for a sentence you say from a reading passage in their textbooks. When found students study the sentence, memorise it and write it on the board when ready. Use the game to work on any grammar, tenses or vocabulary.

There may be a vocabulary index at the back of the class textbook which could be used for this game. If leaders at the board do not spell the word correctly they return to their group and ask for the correct spelling. Optionally students cannot show the leader the word again but spell it out and the leader must memorise the letters. In the case of a sentence the group read out the sentence to the leader who must memorise it and return to the board.

As always an option is deduct any points from a group that is too noisy, or for any groups shouting out corrections to the leader at the board, which is against the rules.

Running Dictation

Category: Listening, writing and spelling
Group size: Up to 30 divided into pairs or groups of 3 to 4
Level: Beginner to Intermediate
Materials: Sentences
Age: 6 to 12
Pace: Wake up

Give a student from each pair a sentence on a piece of paper, or have these students look at a particular sentence from the class textbook. On "Go" students memorise the sentence and go to their partner to dictate the sentence from memory. The partner may write the sentence on the board or at his or her desk if your class is big. Using the same sentence for everyone will make it easy for students to check if they have it right. If a student gets stuck part of the way through the sentence he or she may go back to the written text, read it again and go back to the partner. The first student to have written up the sentence correctly wins.

Organisation of the class

If possible have half of the students at one end and partners at the other. The written text stays at one end of the room so leaders travel back and forth to their partners. However if this would be too chaotic for your classroom then let the students work in pairs side by side. If you do this you structure the timing so leaders cannot simply read out what they have without memorising it. You say, "Go" and give leaders 30 seconds to memorise. You say, "Close books" or "Papers behind backs". Students close the textbook or hold the paper with the sentence on it behind their backs. Allow 30 seconds to a minute for the dictation part. If no student has finished at this point you repeat the above process until one of the partners puts up their hand and asks you to check the sentence. If correct that pair win the point for the round. With a large class, or if you have the same pair winning all the time award points to the first three pairs to come up with a correct sentence. If students feel they have no chance to win a point they will become de-motivated and not want to participate or start to mess around instead of trying. The other thing is to mix up the pairs.

GAMES S

Scissors Paper Stone Pair Work Formation

Category: Speaking
Group size: 4 to 40
Level: Beginner to Advanced
Materials: None
Age: 4 to 12
Pace: Calm

Pair work helps maximise on speaking time. Here is a useful way of organising it. Have the class form two lines facing each other. Each person will perform a pair work exercise with the player opposite, and then, on your signal, everyone moves round one place, the people at the end of the line crossing over to the other side. In this way everyone now has a new partner.

To introduce the "geography" of this exercise play a round of "scissors, paper and stone". Opening the first two fingers into a V forms the scissors; holding the hand flat symbolises the paper while making a fist symbolises the stone.

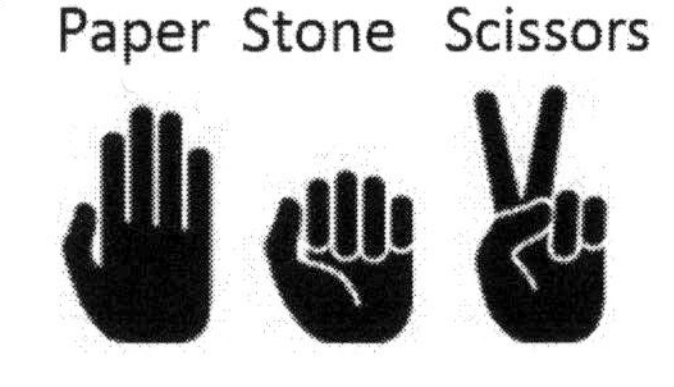

The scissors cut the paper, which wraps the stone, which blunts the scissors. The scissors win over the paper, which wins over the stone, which wins over the scissors. On the count of three both players make and name the symbol for one of the three items.

This will give everyone the hang of the pair work exercise and the moving round each time to a fresh partner. Once you have that down pat use it for any pair work exchange, replacing scissors, paper and stone with a question and answer format, short dialogue, mini interview or the vocabulary and/or grammar you need to work on.

A vocabulary game I saw Sarah Nakel demonstrate in Denmark using Scissors paper stone is as follows. Stick up vocabulary words in a row. Children form two lines. The first two children walk towards each other, touching and naming the vocabulary as they go. Where the children meet, they do scissors paper stone with each other. The winner moves on. The loser stays put. The next children in the line immediately move onto the vocabulary cards, naming them and advancing along the line towards the other side. Wherever two children meet, they do scissors paper stone. When a child has reached the other side he or she goes to the back of the line on that side.

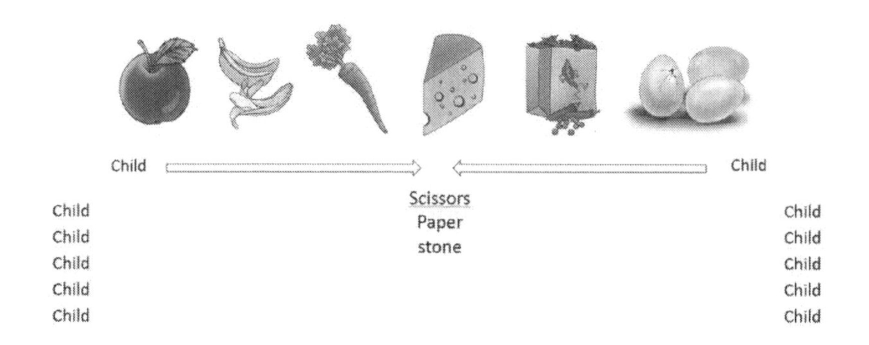

Sentence Conversion

Category: Speaking
Group size: 2 to 30
Level: Flexible for all levels

Materials: Prepared sentences for the teacher
Age: 6 to 12 - keep it simple for the young ones
Pace: Excitable

Divide the class into teams of three. Each team has three players, A, B and C. Send all the Cs down to the far end of the room. Have all the As and Bs at the front and read them a sentence such as "I eat apples". The As walk down to the end of the room and say the sentence to their team member C. C must convert this sentence into the past tense and come up to the front to give you and the Bs the answer: "I ate apples".

Now send the Bs down there and repeat the exercise using a different sentence: "I walk to the bus". The As come back with "I walked to the bus".

Adapt this for any grammar such as converting present continuous to past continuous or past tense to conditional and so on. Always demonstrate with one team first so everyone knows what to do. If players fail to come up with the right answer then you need to do more structured drilling. In this case stop the game and go back to it in another lesson.

Only accept answers from the students whose turn it is. The others must stay in place, touching the wall. This keeps a semblance of order and prevents the teacher from being overwhelmed with enthusiastic children. If noise levels are a problem impose a whispering only rule with deduction of points for offenders.

Shop-A-Holics

Category: Step 4 Speaking drill
Group size: 5 to 30
Level: Beginner to Lower Intermediate
Materials: Picture flashcards or real items and pretend money, which can be paper, coins or any small objects
Age: 4 to 12
Pace: Wake up

In this game pupils pretend to buy things. Make a third to half of the class shopkeepers and the rest shoppers. The shopkeepers can have their backs to the walls of the classroom with pictures of the items they have for sale on a desk. If you have a small group play with real objects if you have them but with a class pictures are more practical. Shoppers each have a set amount of money and must accumulate as many products as possible. The shopkeepers cannot sell anything unless correctly asked for in English. Shoppers have a time limit to buy as many items as they can.

There is a catch. Every so often you announce that one of the products is off and must be recalled. Any students with that item in their basket must hand it over to the teacher and the shopkeepers withdraw it from their shops. Write the item on the board for reference. Anyone found with that item at the end of the game in his or her shopping basket is out.

When the time limit is up students count up the items they have and the winners have the most. In order to have lots of winners say that any student with over five items is a winner. Or say that any students with fewer than ten items must do a funny forfeit. Avoid making it traumatic for the students who have to do the forfeit. One does not want them to feel like they have failed. Children can be so sensitive about winning and losing that one has to tread carefully.

Tips: Give students plenty of money as the idea is to have them shopping and not standing around because they have run out. If you have monopoly money that is fantastic, otherwise use pieces of paper. Possibly ask the children to prepare an A4 sheet of bank notes for homework. Younger children are thrilled when they play with fake money as it makes them feel grown up.

Before you play have two children demonstrate the dialogue you would like exchanged at the shop. With beginners keep it short and simple. As the children will be repeating the same thing over and over this is a drill type game so accuracy is important, therefore it is better to be short and accurate than long-winded, slow and full of errors. Make sure children are properly prepared. For example play a game such as Team Race Question and Answer, where the children ask the question in unison, to drill something like "Could I have some carrots please?" or "How much are the carrots?" Use some step 3 speaking games to drill both the question and answer sides of the dialogue before releasing children to practise together in Shopaholics.

Shopping List Memory Game

Category: Speaking
Group size: Any class size in groups of 2 to 6 players per group
Level: Beginner to Lower Intermediate
Materials: Optional Pictures
Age: 4 to 12
Pace: Calm

How to play – small group variant

Place picture cards of your chosen vocabulary in a pile. Player 1 takes a card and lays it down naming the picture or making a sentence about it as required. Player 2 picks out another card and lays it down next to player 1's picture. Player 2 repeats the required sentence, adding his or her chosen item to the list, and so it goes on, with the list getting longer and longer, for example:

Player 1: In my trolley I have got some milk,

Player 2: In my trolley I have got some milk and some chocolate

Player 3: In my trolley I have got some milk, some chocolate and some oranges

For younger players or when using freshly introduced vocabulary use picture cards as prompts as described above, for older or more advanced players they rely on memory alone.

Language ideas

This game is adaptable to a multitude of language uses, for example:

There is/there are: In my wardrobe there are socks, there are shoes, there is a dress, there are shirts, there is a scarf etc.

Her name is/His name is: Her name is Barbie, his name is Ken, her name is Rita, and his name is Paul etc.

She's a/he's a: She's a model, he's an action man, she's a nurse, he's a doctor, etc.

She likes milk/she does not like tea.

Playing sports: He plays golf, he plays tennis, he goes riding, he windsurfs, etc.

Past tense: Yesterday for supper I had milk, chocolate, pizza, etc.

Months: In December it was windy, in January it was cold and in February it was icy.

Easy, intermediate and advanced variations

For advanced players have them make up and recite a story. An option is to give students a specific tense to work with in the story. Use picture cards for them to weave into the story or not as you like. As the phrases created will be repeated over and over it is worth ensuring they are correct in order to avoid inadvertently reinforcing errors, for that reason this is best as a structured speaking exercise to reinforce a particular grammatical feature rather than a free-speaking exercise. Ask players to write the story up from memory afterwards if you wish.

Another way to play that is more intermediate is to give each child a line of the story. The first player reads out the first line of the story. The second player must memorise it, repeat it and add his or her line. The third player repeats the first two lines and adds a line and so on. Keep the sentences short so that they are easy to remember.

Easy variant good for small and larger groups

This variant can be used with new vocabulary and short sentences. Sit the children in a circle. Start the game saying "one hat". Each child repeats this until it comes back to you. The child next to you then adds one item, "one hat, two gloves", and this goes round the group until it comes back to that child. The next child along adds a third item and so on. Use with any vocabulary.

Show Me

Category: Listening
Group size: 2 to a large class
Level: Beginner to Lower Intermediate
Materials: Classroom items or any items you have to hand
Age: 4 to 12
Pace: Wake up

This is a simple game where the players show their understanding of vocabulary. It allows you to observe how pupils are doing. It is good for introducing new vocabulary or revising it before a speaking game. Ask players to show you an item. For example say, "show me a pen" and everyone holds up a pen. "Show me a blue pen" and students hold up a blue pen. Here are other ideas: show me the floor, the ceiling, the wall, the left wall, the right wall, a rubber, a ruler, a friend, a girl, a boy, a hand, a leg, a friend's foot, a blue skirt, a sock, a door, a pen in a pencil case, a pen under a pencil case and so on for the prepositions, etc.

For a variant give out picture cards so the children hold up the correct picture as you ask for it. Have pupils point to the item on the wall.

Movement variant

If you have the space it is fun to distribute picture or word flash cards around the room. Call out, "show me a pig". All the children run to the picture of the pig. If you have more than 10 children you'll need more than one picture of each item, or you'll find it too crowded, and the group will be too unwieldy, with everyone trying to get close to one little picture.

Silly Dialogues and Stories

Category: Writing, then reading out loud
Group size: 2 to a large class
Level: Any
Materials: None
Age: From 6 to adult
Pace: Calm

The class will write a story or dialogue collectively. Here is an example using a romance. Everyone writes chunks of the story as per your instructions. Start the story with the girl's name and a description of her. Fold the paper over and pass it to the next player. Each player now writes the boy's name, and a description of him, folds the paper and passes it on. Next comes how they met, the first words the boy said to the girl, how the girl replied to the boy, what happened next, what the neighbour said, the consequences, what the newspapers said, and their future. When everyone has finished unfold the papers and read some of the funny stories aloud. Stick the others on the walls for children to read at their leisure in between class. Some of the dialogues will make sense and some will be funny. A challenging option is to get each pair to work on their dialogue or story and turn it into something that makes sense or act it out convincingly.

Other scenarios

A salesman comes to the door to sell an item. The conversation talks about what he is selling, what the item is used for, where would you put it in the house and how much it is. This could lead to incongruous conversations where a lady buys some encyclopedias that she keeps in the garden shed to clean her bath.

A patient goes to the doctor. The conversation talks about which body part hurts and how the patient got injured. The doctor asks to examine the body part and gives the remedy. This could lead to incongruous conversations where a patient has a broken elbow, injured while cycling so the doctor asks to examine his leg and prescribes an antibiotic.

A customer orders food in a restaurant. The waiter brings the dish. The customer finds a foreign object in the food. The waiter proposes a solution. The customer accepts or rejects the solution.

Simon Says

Category: Listening
Group size: 2 to a large class
Level: Beginners to Lower Intermediate
Materials: None
Age: 4 to Adult
Pace: Wake up

Simon says is an extremely useful classroom game, and can be adapted to a wide age range, becoming increasingly sophisticated as the players get older or have a greater command of the language. The classic version of Simon Says is as follows: The teacher starts off as Simon and gives the players instructions which they must follow, but only if Simon says so. For example:

"Simon says touch your nose." Simon touches his nose and all players touch their nose.

"Simon says touch your feet." Simon touches his feet and all players touch their feet.

"Touch your head." Simon touches his head but players must not touch their head since Simon didn't say so. Any players touching their head lose a life.

Normally in the classic version any players who touched their head would be out however it is better to make them lose a life, as the idea is to have everyone playing, not sitting around watching. Alternatively as soon as you have three people out you restart the game with everyone playing again, and with a big class that is a good way to go because the more children you have the harder it is to keep track of lost lives.

Language ideas

Obviously Simon Says is a great game for body parts, and once your players have got the hang of the vocabulary they can be Simon. However the language potential for Simon Says does not stop there. Here are some other examples of things that Simon can say:

- Raise your left hand/Touch your right leg
- Touch something blue
- Touch different articles of clothing
- Touch a body part of the person next to you
- Jump/run/skip/stop/dance/sing/be silent/sit down/stand up/listen/look at the ceiling/look up/look down/look to the left/look at the floor/touch a chair/write/
- Mime an animal
- Mime an action such as drink a glass of water/eat an ice cream/sleep/ get dressed/ get undressed/pretend to be a model/pretend to be Batman/Spiderman
- Jump on a picture - lay out pictures on the floor for players to become familiar with or revise specific vocabulary. Simon says Jump on the train! Jump on the bus!
- Touch a real object - spread out objects that the players touch on Simon's instruction. Touch the train/the car/the plane if you have toy versions of these for example, or use pictures if not.

Harder versions of Simon Says

For players with a good command of the language, and once they have got Simon Says down pat, complicate the game to keep them on their toes. In this version Simon says two things at once, for example:

Simon says raise your hand and Simon says touch your leg

The players must raise their hand and touch their leg

Simon says eat ice-cream and touch your nose

The players must eat ice cream but not touch their nose because Simon did not say so.

And here is a third, even more complicated version and you might need to rehearse being Simon for this one!

When Simon says to do something the players have to keep doing it until Simon specifically asks them to stop. In the meantime Simon continues to make other requests. For example:

- Simon says touch your head
- Simon says touch your shoulder and Simon says stick your tongue out
- Simon says spin around and shout JUMP!
- At this point the players should be spinning round with one hand on their head and the other on their shoulder, sticking their tongue out, but they should not shout JUMP, as Simon did not say to do so.
- Simon then continues with: Simon says stop touching your head and rub your stomach instead

Players must stop touching their heads but should not rub their stomachs, as Simon did not say so.

Well I'm sure you get the picture. This game is a lot of fun and the trick is for you as Simon to keep the pace up and link the commands rapidly so your players' attention is absolutely riveted on listening to your every word!

There is nothing to prevent you playing until you have a winner. The better you get at being Simon the sooner you will trick everyone into making a mistake and you have a winner fairly quickly, before those who are out have time to get bored. So that it is easy for you to see who is still in the game have those who are out sit down. I have seen this played with 8000 adults at a seminar and the game lasted less than five minutes before everyone was out!

Simon says speaking variant

Allow your players to be Simon. There could be several Simons at once, as while one Simon is giving a command the other can be thinking of the next one - this ensures the pace is fast and furious, which it needs to be to make this game really fun.

Sit and Be Silent

Category: No category – a game to retain order and quiet quickly
Group size: any
Level: all levels
Materials: none
Age: 4 to 12
Pace: wake up

At the beginning of the term or lesson explain the game to the children and say that this game could happen at any time during the lesson and in any subsequent lessons. Establish a signal that means this game is commencing. Turning the lights on and off is a good one as that is a visual clue rather than a loud noise that would have to be heard over the potential din of a speaking activity. Another clue could be that the teacher puts on a special hat or goes to a specific spot in class and performs a specific action.

When the teacher gives the signal the game is on. It is quite simply that the last person to be sitting down with forefinger on lips in silence is the loser. This could mean doing a forfeit, disqualifying that team from the game in play when Sit and Be Silent starts.

When you give the signal make sure some students see you do it so they at least sit and are silent. Gradually other students will see this happening and cotton on to the game. Then you will get a rush of students returning to their seats to be silent. Hopefully you will not often have a loser but will have many students sitting down simultaneously, which lets you off the hook of showing up the last child. Anyway it is not obligatory to have a penalty, with everyone now sitting continue with the next activity.

Snowballs

Category: Reading and speaking – good end of term game
Group size: 2 to 20 or more although it will be increasingly chaotic
Level: Beginner to Intermediate
Materials: Questions written out on individual pieces of paper and screwed up into snowballs

Age: 4 to 12
Pace: Excitable

This is a good game to use in a last lesson of the term. It is useful but also great fun. Write out one question on a piece of paper for every member of your class. Use scrap paper otherwise this is a total waste of resources. Newspapers are great for scrunching. Either scrunch these papers up yourself or give out the sheets in class and ask the students to screw them up lightly. It is important that they are not scrunched hard as they will be repeatedly unfolded, read and scrunched up again, so you do not want to crush them totally. If you have the students do the scrunching that will save you time and will mean that the papers are easier to transport into class. Another option is to let the students write out the questions themselves from a selection that you put on the board.

Now each student holds a ball of paper with a question. On your command students throw their ball at another student. If the ball hits the student he or she must pick it up, unfold it and answer the question on the sheet. If the student answers the question correctly he or she earns a point. Alternatively students who cannot answer the question have to do a forfeit.

In order to avoid total chaos it is best to have four or five students having a turn at one time while the rest sit quietly. Students who will throw the ball stand. Students who are hit must stand, read the question out loud and answer it. If a student does not hit any student with the snowball allow another turn.

Warn students that any violent throwing will not be tolerated. Use the Sit and Be Silent Game to retain quiet and order quickly when you need it.

Spell and Act

Category: Listening
Group size: 2 to 40
Level: Beginner to Advanced
Materials: None
Age: 6 to 12

Pace: Calm

Spell out a word such as "s a d", and your players mime it. Spell out sentences or say a part of the sentence and spell the key word, for example, "I play t-e-n-n-i-s". Allow the younger players to write the letters down as you go, as they may have trouble visualising the word. Players may spell words out for another team to name. If players find it difficult allow them to write down their own words and then spell them out.

Spell and Speak

Category: Speaking
Group size: 2 to 30
Level: Lower Intermediate to Advanced
Materials: None
Age: 8 to 12
Pace: Calm

This game works in the same way as Spell and Act. Put players into teams and spell out a word such as "l-i-g-h-t" or "p-l-o-u-g-h". As soon as a player has identified the word, whether or not you have finished spelling it out, they knock on their desk and give you the answer, gaining points if correct. With more advanced players this is quite a good game to highlight certain words such as "bow" which can be pronounced in two different ways, with different meanings, and which can be a noun and a verb (a bow, to bow).

This game to draws attention to words which have silent letters, (as in "light" and "plough") or pairs of sounds with different spellings, (such as whine and "wine", heel and heal, whether and weather, den and when, graph and staff) or words which are frequently misspelled, (such as recommend, apartment, principle, principal or exercise).

Give your class a homework assignment where each person prepares a list of 3 words they find difficult to spell. Put the class into teams and have them play Spell and Speak with their own selection of words.

Spelling Board Game and Variants

Category: Spelling
Group size: 2 to a class with children working in pairs or small groups
Level: Beginner to Intermediate
Materials: Words and optional use of board games
Age: 6 to adult
Pace: Calm

Board game variant

If you have some board games already as part of your teaching resources use any one with dice so players can advance around the board. The first player rolls the dice. Another player turns over a word card from a pile without showing this to the others and reads out the word. The first player spells this word and if correct advances around the board by the number of squares shown on the dice. If incorrect the first player is shown the correct spelling and cannot move his piece that turn. Continue until one of the players makes it all the way round the board. A variant to include more players is for all players to write out the word and all those who are correct advance round the board.

Board games are included with the stories and lesson plan series here: www.teachingenglishgames.com/esl-stories-for-children.

Variant with no board game

If you do not have access to any board games or dice play this variant. The children have a pile of word cards face down on the table. One player turns over a card and reads out the word. Player 1 must spell this out. If correct, player 1 keeps the card as a point. Turns are taken around the circle so everyone has the same number of goes. The winner is the one with the most cards at the end. It is discouraging to lose all the time so be careful to mix good students in with weaker ones.

Collaborative variant

This can be played as a collaborative game too. Each group is a team competing against other groups. One player reads out a word. Another player writes that word down and if spelled correctly the group keep that card as a point. If the player misspells the word the card is placed back in the pile and the pile is shuffled so the students have a chance to spell it again correctly when it reappears at the top of the pile.

After a given amount of time the game is stopped and the group with the most points at that moment wins. Groups can justify their points by showing the teacher the list of correctly spelled words. If you think that cheating is a problem with this game simply make one member of the group a representative from another team. This person will read out the words and will not give the spelling away as the group members are not on his or her team.

If noise is a problem specify that this game is to be played in English only and any use of the native language that the teacher hears will mean immediate confiscation of a point from that team.

Spoon Game

Category: Speaking vocabulary drill
Group size: up to 15
Level: Beginner
Materials: playing cards and spoons
Age: 6 to 12
Pace: Lively

This is a summer camp or end of term game. You need four matching cards per player such as 4 tens, 4 jacks, 4 queens, 4 kings and 4 aces, making 20 cards for 5 players. Multiply the number of sets of 4 according to the number of players. You also need one less spoon than the number of players, so 4 spoons for 5 players. Shuffle and deal out the cards. Scatter the spoons in the center of the group.

Choose two vocabulary words such as “cabbages and onions”. On “cabbages” everyone passes a card to the left. On “onions” players pick up the card on their right. Players quickly decide which card keep and which to pass on, the idea being to collect four of the same. This game is very fast. Some players are faffing with their cards when others have already passed on a card. But everyone must pass on “onions” whether ready or not.

When a player has four matching cards (4 aces, 4 jacks etc.) he or she takes a spoon from the middle of the table. As soon as one person has taken a spoon anyone can take one, regardless of the cards in his or her hand. What happens is a mad rush to grab a spoon and someone is always left empty-handed since there is one less spoon. When the first player takes a spoon he or she may do so discreetly. Some will notice and quietly take a spoon but others will carry on playing until suddenly everyone notices and rushes for the remaining spoons. One has to watch the game as well as the cards.

Change the vocabulary words for each round. Keep up a rhythm, it’s a fast game. There are no penalties or score-keeping. It is not necessary but you could have forfeits for the person who doesn’t have a spoon.

Spot the Difference

Category: Writing
Group size: any
Level: Beginner to Intermediate
Materials: Two similar but not identical pictures
Age: 6 to 12
Pace: Calm

Prepare in advance, or on the board, two identical pictures and either colour them in different colours, or make some changes to one of them. Show the first picture only for a few minutes and then cover it up and show the second picture. Your pupils must write down the differences.

A way to obtain two similar pictures easily could be to use a web cam that is broadcasting such as a tourist office website like www.valdisere.com. Save the image in the morning and then again at night. The background will be the same but there will be differences in the people in the image, the time of day and what is happening. Depending on the level, and whether or not you are revising or practising relatively new language, I suggest writing up a few fill in the blanks type sentences on the board as a prompt. For example draw a picture of a cowboy, and in the second picture draw the same cowboy but with a pink hat, a feather and some different coloured pointy boots. On the board you write: The cowboy _ _ _ wearing a ___________, now he _ _ _ _ _ _ _ _ _ _ _ a _____________. The pupils fill in: The cowboy was wearing a black hat, now he is wearing a pink hat.

With clothing bring in real items and play Dress Up as well as this game. Bring two or more students to the front, put a few items on them, let the class look at them for a minute, send them out and give them 30 seconds to swap over their items or put on some different items, and then come back in for the class to spot the differences and write them down as outlined above.

Squeak Piggy Squeak!

Category: Speaking
Group size: 4 to 20
Level: Beginner to Lower Intermediate
Materials: A cushion and blindfold
Age: 4 to 10 and possibly older if not too 'cool' for the game
Pace: Wake up

To play you need enough room for everyone to sit on the floor as this game cannot be played with chairs. Piggy would have a long way to fall if he missed the person's lap.

Sit pupils in a circle with the piggy standing in the middle, blindfolded and holding a cushion. With more than 8 players have two piggies in the middle, each blindfolded and with a cushion, three piggies for 15 children and four for 20. On your signal, the piggies make their way cautiously towards the edge of the circle and sit down on their cushion, in the lap of one of the players. In the classic party game the piggy says "squeak piggy squeak", the player goes "oink oink", and the piggy tries to guess who he or she is sitting on but replace the oinks with any language. For example use a question and answer format with the player replying using a funny voice as a disguise. The piggy can have people count from one to ten, name three objects in the room, describe what they are wearing, etc.

Stop!

Category: Writing and speaking
Group size: 2 to 40
Level: Beginner to Intermediate
Materials: Pen and paper
Age: 8 to 12
Pace: Calm

All players draw a chart with 5 or 6 columns, each with a heading, such as numbers, names, countries, animals, clothes, professions, TV shows, food, fruits, things they would like to have, etc. Use headings the players have plenty of vocabulary in. One of the players starts the game by calling out the letters of the alphabet. The player next to him or her randomly calls out "Stop!" The one saying the letters of the alphabet has to stop on whatever letter has just been said. Everyone now writes down an item in each category starting with that letter. The first person to finish says "Stop!" Everyone has to stop writing, whether finished or not.

If no one has said stop after one minute, perhaps because everyone is having difficulty thinking up words beginning with the chosen letter, say stop yourself so the game does not drag. Continue for a few rounds and review the answers, awarding a point for each word written. If someone has a word that no one else has award double points for being original. Have all players call out their answers so the children hear the vocabulary repeatedly. Children tick off their words when they are called out. Either trust the players to do their own scores or have them swap papers with someone else. Here is an example of a player's chart:

Animals	**Countries or continents**	**Professions**	**Colours**
Panda	Poland	Priest	Purple
Snake	South America	Singer	Silver

This game requires good vocabulary and beginners will have lots of gaps in their charts. This doesn't matter as long as you keep up a rapid pace, moving on to a fresh letter rather than agonizing to find words when the vocabulary range just isn't there. Get around this limitation by using much broader categories such as nouns, verbs and names rather than countries, clothes and furniture. Also make sure categories chosen are age appropriate. Countries will be difficult for younger children. More challenging categories are educational in the wider sense, such as composers and musical instruments, so these are worth working on with older students.

GAMES T

Team Race – Listening Version

Category: Listening
Group size: 1 to 30 divided into teams
Level: Beginner to Advanced
Materials: Pictures
Age: 4 to 12
Pace: Wake up to Excitable

This is played exactly as Team Race Question and Answer (see below) except that there is no speaking. Use this to drill vocabulary so students hear and recognize new words. The players are divided into their teams ready to go. Call out the word and the first players run down, collect the relevant picture and run back. They join the back of their team's line and wait for their turn to come around again.

Team Race Question and Answer

Category: Speaking - asking short questions and learning new vocabulary

Group size: 2 to a class of 30 divided into teams
Level: Beginner to Advanced
Materials: Pictures
Age: 4 to 12
Pace: Wake up to Excitable

How to play

Place a pile of picture cards at the end of the room and have all players line up behind a line. The players ask you a question in unison, such as "What do you do?" and you answer, "I'm a dentist". As soon as players hear your answer they run down to the pile of pictures and pick out the picture of the dentist. There is only one picture of each profession so only one player will return with a picture. However you may choose to have enough copies of the dentist for each player to return with a card as a variation. This is better for 4 to 6 year olds who may be upset to return empty handed.

With four players make two teams of 2, or with six players, two teams of 3 etc. The maximum team size should be not more than six players per team, more and the team members get bored or distracted waiting for a turn. With a class of 18 it is better to have six teams of 3 than two teams of 9 for example. With a class of thirty have six teams of 5, with two piles of picture cards at the end of the room, three teams running to each pile. This avoids having too many players running for the same place causing a general pile-up and too much of a scramble. Once the first players have run to the pictures and back they join the back of their team's line and wait until it is their turn again.

The game continues until all the pictures have been collected and everyone has had at least one go. Then swap team members around and play again. Regularly re-mix teams as this shares the winning around.

Uneven team numbers are no problem. Players line up behind each other in their teams and the last player races against the first player from the other team. Or have a player be a caller instead of you, to give someone more speaking opportunity.

Variant contributed by a teacher: This is how I play your game with my students; I write down different sentences which I have taught my students on cards with their names at the back. I divide my students into two groups. I put the cards into two different baskets about 15 meters from where they stand. I call out their names, for example Rose and Mike, they run to the baskets looking for their names and read out loud the question on the card, after that they run back to shake the hands of their partners next in line who must answer the question, and then also run to the basket looking for their names and read out their question.

Language ideas

The game can be used with as many question and answer forms as you have imagination. Here are some examples:
Clothing: What are you wearing? I'm wearing...trousers!
Past tense: Where did you go on holiday? I went to the beach
Weather: What's the weather like? It's raining.
Professions: What do you do? I'm a doctor
The time: What time is it? It's one o'clock
Age and numbers: How old are you? 'I'm 10
Sports and past tense: What did you do this weekend? I played tennis

Substitute word flash cards instead of picture cards if you do not have any pictures, although using pictures is better for working with vocabulary.

Shopping variant

Divide the group into teams of not more than 6 per team. One member of each team, designated as the shop assistant, goes down the other end of the room and stands behind a desk with either real items, or picture cards on it. If you have no desk, just place the items or picture cards on the floor. Give each team a basket or bag (optional) and a shopping list made of pictures or words. If your shopping lists are different you will be able to play more than once.

Line the teams up at the start and say, "Ready, steady, go!" The first team member runs down to the shop. The shop assistant says, "Hello, what would you like?" (Or "what can I get you", or whatever phrase of this type you are teaching). The team member replies by asking for one of the items on his or her list, using "I'd like..." Leave out the shop assistant's question if you prefer.

Team Race on the Board

Category: Listening
Group size: 2 to 30 divided into teams
Level: Beginner to Advanced
Materials: Class board and pens
Age: 5 to 12
Pace: Wake up to Excitable

This is played in the same way as Team Race Question and Answer but using the class board instead of pictures. If the class is seated at desks in rows make each row from the front to back of the class a team. Then call out a number and the first member from each team runs up to the board and writes up that number. Alternatively have pupils run up and draw the item you name, rub out an item you name or write up a word. The team can be allowed to help out and correct the spelling if necessary.

The class, or just the players concerned, can ask a question before you give out the instruction. For example students ask in unison: What do we write at the speed of light? Make up any silly chant containing grammar you wish to drill or use a question, and make it easier or harder depending on the age and level of your class.

The Big Freeze

Category: Listening
Group size: 2 to a large class
Level: Beginner to Intermediate
Materials: None

Age: 4 to 12
Pace: Calm

Have all your players walk around the room. For large classes where it is not feasible for children to leave their desks have them move their arms, fingers, heads, feet and bodies slowly while standing still. Tell a story, sing a song or randomly say a number of words while pupils listen intently and whenever they hear a specified word or phrase they freeze. If they move they are out. For example you could say that whenever they hear an item of clothing they must freeze, or a type of food, or a profession, or a specific phrase. Your story can be nonsense, and it doesn't matter if the players understand all of it, or even any of it, as they are listening out for the special words. It is nice if you tell a real story, but it is not an obligation to play the game.

A variant on this is instead of freezing pupils clap their hands above their heads - this allows you to keep up a faster pace instead of stopping for prolonged periods to see if anyone is moving. For 4 to 6 year olds and as a variant for all ages, they can sit down whenever they hear the word and all try not to be the last one sitting down.

Optionally tell your story or say your words in a rap rhythm, or play a song (make sure one can actually hear the words in it though), and ask the players to listen out for certain words, so if you played Sting's "Every breath you take" you could have the players listen out for "watching, heart, baby, please, breath". With a younger audience you would want to choose songs for their age group such as Old MacDonald Had A Farm.

Spelling game

This may also be used as a spelling game. Say a word such as cat and then spell it out. If you spell it correctly the children keep moving, if you spell it wrong the children freeze or clap.

The Blanket Game

Category: Speaking
Group size: Variants for all class sizes from 2 up
Level: Beginner to Lower Intermediate
Materials: A sheet or blanket. Variant with no materials
Age: 4 to 12
Pace: Calm

First create a barrier for someone to hide behind. Do this by setting up a clothes line and pegging a blanket on it, by having two students hold the blanket up, or by draping the blanket over a couple of chairs so someone could sit behind it and not be seen. Now you have your barrier, here is an example of how to play this using clothing vocabulary: A child hides behind the blanket and puts on a selection of clothes, or props, such as a hat, belt, tie or scarf. The class asks in unison, "What are you wearing?" The person behind the blanket replies, "I'm wearing a hat" or "I'm wearing a red hat". Each student decides whether he or she thinks this is true or false.

Whoever thinks it is true stands up. Whoever thinks it is false sits down. Now the person behind the blanket reveals whether or not he is wearing a red hat. (Use real clothes or use pictures of clothes). If a red hat is correct then all those who sat down are out and only those standing up are in. If it's not a red hat, but a black coat, then those standing up are out and have to sit down while those sitting down, who are still in, stand up again for the next round.

Another way to play is for each class member to hold up a paper with either a "True" or "False" on it. Everyone starts the game standing up. The person behind the blanket chooses whether or not to wear the red hat and students hold up either a True or a False card. Then everyone who got it wrong sits down and stays seated while you play the next rounds until you only have a few students standing. You may also play with a tick and a cross rather than the words true and false, which is easier for the younger ones.

Continue, and then swap over the person behind the blanket. Only allow that pupil a few seconds to dress up, to ensure that the others do not get bored waiting. The class can count up to thirty or say the alphabet while the person puts their prop on. If there are only 2 of you - you and your student - then you take it in turns to go behind the blanket. Dressing up is only one idea for this game to work with clothing vocabulary and related short questions and sentences such as "What are you wearing?" Alternatively use flashcards instead of props.

Simple vocabulary repetition variant – small class

For elementary levels, or to revise vocabulary place two pictures (or word cards) on the floor behind the blanket – for example a picture of a plane and a truck. A pupil stands on one of the cards and says "plane", or a sentence such as "I'm going to Paris by plane". The student may stand either on the plane or the truck and the class must guess whether what he or she says is true or false as described above.

Simple vocabulary repetition variant – large class

If you have a fairly big class then you will not have time for everyone to go behind the blanket, so in that case, to get the most out of the time spent, instead of the person behind the blanket saying "plane", have your class say "plane" or "truck" depending on which one they think their class mate is standing on. Once the person behind the blanket is on their chosen picture you say "Ready, Go!" and the class call out the picture they think is correct. They may also call out the sentence you are requiring them to drill. That way everyone has a chance to say the words, rather than just the person behind the blanket. Students award themselves points if they get it right. Some of the children will cheat and pretend they said the right word – but does it really matter? After all we only want them to speak English and feel good about it.

Question drill variant

This isn't a true or false variant, but while we've got the blanket out we might as well use it to the full. Put one class member behind the blanket along with a few picture or word cards. Lay out 3 to 4 picture cards for the young children, and up to twelve for older children. The words should all be in the same theme and if you need to have a set of these cards in view of the class. With older children you would probably not do this to make it more challenging for them. Allow the child behind the blanket five seconds to select a picture to stand on. He or she now cannot move from that spot. See below for how to continue depending on whether you have a large or small class.

Question drill – large class

Display pictures or write the words you are using. One pupil comes up to the front and points at one of the words – for example the car. The class ask the question form in unison, such as "Have you got a car?" The person behind the blanket replies, "Yes I have" if standing on the car and "no I haven't" if standing on another picture. The class see how many questions they need to ask before discovering the picture the person behind the blanket is standing on. Alternatively divide students into two teams and each team tries to guess in fewer goes than the other one.

Question or sentence drill – small class

Each class member in turn asks a question and hopes to be the one to guess correctly. For example, the first student asks, "Have you got a car?" Answer, "No, I haven't". The second student asks, "Have you got a plane?" and so on until the answer is "Yes I have." Give points if you wish. If you only have one or two students then join in the game with them. Adapt this game to ask any question. Choose a question form and then pick some vocabulary that goes well with that question form.

A lively variant

Here is a livelier variant of this game for smaller classes: One child goes behind the blanket and the class says this rhyme together quickly and rhythmically if possible.

What is it? What is it? What could it be?

What is it? What is it? One, two, three.

It helps if the children clap on the 'what', 'what', 'what' and 'be' and on 'what', 'what', 'one', and 'three'. By the time the class reach 'three' the person behind the blanket MUST be standing on their chosen card. After the class have pronounced the word three they are free to call out any possible word. Each class member can only call out one word but they can all call their words out together. There will be some noise! As soon as the child behind the blanket hears the correct word they jump out and all those who called out that word award themselves points (mass cheating no doubt, not to worry). The next child to go behind the blanket heads over there while the class immediately start up the rhyme again. The pace should be fast and exciting with no time in between rounds.

Replace the simple rhyme above with one that you make up, which may include the sentence or question structure you need to teach, or it may be a rhyme with some vocabulary you would like to reinforce. Here is an example:

Travel on a bus

Travel on a train

Ride on a bicycle

Fly in a plane

When played well, this game is pretty noisy and fun, and the children have a chance to repeat the same words over and over so they will remember them.

You might want to teach the rhyme in a previous lesson, and use it again in other games. The first time you play start slowly, gradually picking up the pace.

Tongue Twisters

Category: Speaking
Group size: Any
Level: Intermediate to Advanced

Materials: None
Age: 6 upward
Pace: Wake up

1. Give out the tongue twisters as anagrams and let the class work out the sentences.
2. Dictate the tongue twister in a monotone with no punctuation and let the class work out the punctuation and meaning.
3. Use tongue twisters in Chinese Whispers or Relay Race

Here are some classic tongue twisters to have fun with.

Peter Piper picked a pick of pickled peppers, a pick of pickled peppers Peter Piper picked.

She sells seashells on the seashore.
The shells she sells are seashells.

I wish to wish the wish you wish to wish, but if you wish the wish the witch wishes, I won't wish the wish you wish to wish.

Betty bought butter but the butter was bitter, so Betty bought better butter to make the bitter butter better.

Fuzzy Wuzzy was a bear, Fuzzy Wuzzy had no hair, Fuzzy Wuzzy wasn't very fuzzy, was he?

If a black bug bleeds black blood, what colour blood does a blue bug bleed?

It's not the cough that carries you off;
it's the coffin they carry you off in!

I saw a saw that could out saw any saw I ever saw before.

Any noise annoys an oyster but a noisy noise annoys an oyster more.

More advanced tongue twisters
Mr. See owned a saw. And Mr. Soar owned a seesaw.
Now See's saw sawed Soar's seesaw before Soar saw See, which made Soar sore.
Had Soar seen See's saw before See sawed Soar's seesaw; See's saw would not have sawed Soar's seesaw.

I cannot bear to see a bear bear down upon a hare.
When bare of hair he strips the hare, right there I cry, "Forbear!"

A tree toad loved a she-toad who lived up in a tree.
He was a two-toed tree toad but a three-toed toad was she.
The two-toed tree toad tried to win the three-toed she-toad's heart, for the two-toed tree toad loved the ground that the three-toed tree toad trod.
But the two-toed tree toad tried in vain.
He couldn't please her whim.
From her tree toad bower with her three-toed power the she-toad vetoed him.

Treasure Hunt

Category: Speaking or writing
Group size: 2 to 40
Level: Lower Intermediate to Advanced
Materials: Pictures
Age: 4 to 12
Pace: Wake Up

Scatter pictures all around the classroom, on tables, on chairs and under things. It is a good idea to establish that no pictures are to be put inside bags, as you do not want people riffling through someone else's possessions and potentially scattering them all over the place. Read out a clue for one of the items, adapted to the age and language ability of your group. For example if the item is a television clues could be, "you sit in front of this at home" or

"you watch it" or "home entertainment" or "a tool for communication". If the item is a clock clues could be "It tells the time. It's one o'clock". Use very easy clues with the 4-5 year olds such as, "It's white, it's a drink and you have it with cereals".
As soon as they hear the clue the players look around for the matching item. Give a one-minute time span during which time players who find the item make a note of it against number 1 (for clue number 1). You then read out clue number 2. With a big class not everyone will get round all the pictures in the minute given and that is all part of the game. Students then get together in pairs and check answers with each other, which can only be done through speaking. Students cannot look at each other's papers.

A simpler idea to the clues is simply to call out a word and let the students find its opposite, or its definition. For example, find the opposite of black. Answer: white. Find the definition of dress. Answer: item of clothing.

Writing idea: Have the class work in small groups to come up with a series of clues and items for another team to guess. Then have a play off and see who has the best clues and who can answer them.

True or False

Category: Listening
Group size: 2 to a large class
Level: Beginner to Lower Intermediate
Materials: None, items optional
Age: 4 to 12
Pace: Calm

Name an item or make a statement and the class says whether it is true or false. For example point to a picture of an apple and say "pear", the class must say "False". Hold a pen under a chair and say, "The pen is under the chair", the class must say, "True", etc. Use more sophisticated language such as, "Mary would have gone to the beach but her friends didn't invite her". If you said this while pointing to a beach the answer would be true, but if you were pointing to a picture of a building that would be false.

Truth or Consequence

Category: Reading questions and giving answers
Group size: 2 to 30
Level: Beginner to Intermediate
Materials: Questions in a bucket or bag
Age: 4 to 12
Pace: Wake up

Here you have a list of trivia questions or daft questions written out on cards and placed in a "Question" bucket. Each player picks a question, reads it out and answers it. If the player cannot answer it he or she picks a card from a "Consequence" bucket, which is full of forfeits. This game can be played with any age - you just adapt the difficulty of the questions accordingly, for example: What's 1 plus 2? What is the naughtiest thing you ever did? Who is Mickey Mouse's girlfriend? Name a long yellow fruit. Show a picture and ask, what's this?

With a class of 30 have several children down at the front together reading their questions and answering them. Children can answer individually but while waiting for their turn they can at least be forming the answer in their minds to avoid a lot of hanging around waiting for students to reply. Then do a group forfeit for those who could not answer correctly.

A way of involving more children is to make teams and if a team member has to do a forfeit then the whole team also do it.

Twister

Category: Listening - ideal for body parts and colours
Group size: Small group activity
Level: Beginner to Lower Intermediate
Materials: One Twister sheet per group (none needed for variant)
Age: 4 to 12

Pace: Wake up

Twister is good for exposure to colours and body parts. Buy or make a Twister sheet. To make it take an old sheet and paint circles on it of different colours using some kind of permanent marker pen.

Tell player number 1 to put his right foot on red - he must keep his right foot on red for the duration of the game, player 2 puts her left hand on blue, player 3 puts his left knee on yellow, etc. Continue by adding a body part and a colour each time while your group become progressively more intertwined and stretched into an unbelievable human tangle. If your group do not yet know body parts have pupils touch a colour using any body part they like. Twister sheets can also be used for Musical Vocabulary.

Variant of Twister - needs no material

Play a version of Twister where instead of touching coloured circles people touch someone's hand and someone's leg, and get themselves into a tangle that way. One way of doing this is to divide your class into groups of 12 and each group of 12 into 3 groups of 4 named A, B and C. Tell the class to decide who is A, who is B and who is C. Then tell all the As to touch someone's elbow with their left hand, all the Bs to touch someone's foot with their right hand, and so on, until the As, Bs are Cs and all touching two body parts each. If you want to go on then have them touch another body part, or all sit down while still touching the part, and so on until you have had enough.

GAMES U-Z

Up Jenkins

Category: Speaking - fun question and answer game for small groups
Group size: 6 to 15
Level: Beginner to Lower Intermediate
Materials: A coin and children seated round a table
Age: 4 to 12
Pace: Wake up

Form two teams and choose a captain of each team. The teams sit facing each other along or around a table. Team 1 pass the coin back and forth under the table. The object is for Team 2 opposite to lose track of who has the coin. At any moment the captain of Team 2 may call out "Hands Up!" At this point all members of Team 1 hold their hands above their heads with fists clenched. Team 2's captain then calls out "Hands Down!" and Team 1 must slap their hands down on the table taking care not to make a noise with the coin against the table. Team 2 then have two guesses at who is holding the coin.

Members of Team 2 take it in turns to guess. The designated player from Team 2 asks the person he or she thinks has the coin a question. The person from Team 1 answers and must lift both hands up to show if the coin is on the table. If the coin has not been revealed then a second member of Team 2 may ask a question to a member of Team 1. With 12 to 15 children you might like to allow up to four questions to find the coin. After all from a teacher's perspective it is more useful for the children to be asking and answering questions than passing coins.

Optionally award points to the teams for correct guesses, and for correctly formed questions and answers. You could set a time limit for play, the winning team being the one with the most points when the time limit is up. Make sure all children participate in asking the questions. Alternatively have the whole team ask the question in unison each time for an easy drill.

Upside Down Game

Category: Listening
Group size: Small group at a table or on the floor or a small class
Level: Beginner to Lower Intermediate
Materials: Pictures
Age: 4 to 12
Pace: Calm to Wake up

Place a selection of picture or word cards on the floor or table face up. For a simple vocabulary drill name a word and two students. Those students race to turn over the card you named so it is face down. For a drill to introduce new grammar or reinforce a sentence structure use a sentence containing one of the words visible.

This can then be played in reverse where students turn the cards over that are face down back up again by attempting to remember where the correct word is. If the group is too big then play this with the cards stuck to the board as a demonstration and then split the class and play in small groups. The better students each head a group and take the teacher's role.

Very Large Class Choral Work

Category: Speaking

Group size: Large Classes
Level: Beginner to Lower Intermediate
Materials: None Age: 4 to 12
Pace: Calm to Wake up

Ask the class a series of questions to reinforce any question structure. For example, "Do you play tennis?" The class respond together with either "Yes I do", or "No I don't". If their answer is yes they stand up, and if it is no they sit down, or stay seated. Next ask, "Do you play football", and so on. Then divide the class, half asking questions in unison while the other half answer them. Hold up a picture of a football as the prompt for the children to ask, "Do you like football?"

Vocabulary Cut Outs

Category: Writing
Group size: Any
Level: Beginner to Intermediate
Materials: Cut outs of nouns
Age: 4 to 12
Pace: Calm

This game takes some preparing so I recommend demonstrating the concept to children with a few cut outs of your own and then ask them to each make one or two for homework and bring them in to you.

Print out any flashcard onto 220-gram card and cut around the object. Show the card to students with the white face showing so they only see the outline or shape but not the picture. The idea is to guess what objects these outlines represent. If you hold the cards up to the light they may be see-through so it's best to stick them on the board, especially if the board is white.

Number the back of each picture or keep a track of the order you show them in. Show each outline for a second or so while students write down the name of the item, or guess at it. To help out give clues, such as, this is a sport's item, or this is something you find in the bathroom. Students swap over their lists and you then show the real pictures.

Vocabulary Revision Snap

Category: Speaking Drill
Group size: Table top game for groups of 2 to 6 players
Level: Beginner
Materials: Major preparation required for the card sets but these can be re-used for life if laminated
Age: 4 to 12
Pace: Wake up

This is a basic vocabulary drill game that is excellent to finish a lesson or use on a summer camp. The card sets are elaborate to make and should be done by the children, one card each as a homework task. Scan these in colour, print and laminate for lifelong sets.

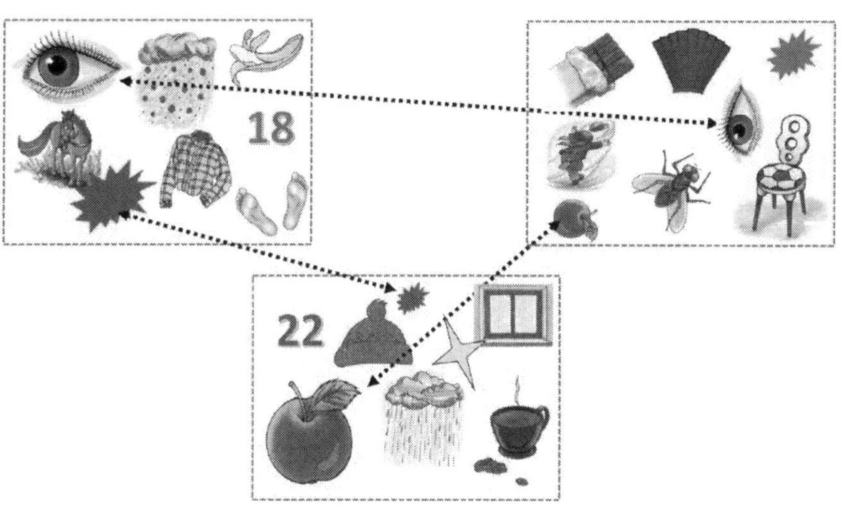

A set with 55 objects distributed over 55 cards with 8 objects per card is included with the flashcards and printable extras available here:

www.teachingenglishgames.com/flashcards

Simpler sets can be made with four objects per card and sticking to a particular vocabulary theme.

How to play

Shuffle the cards and deal out one card to each player face down. Place the other cards in a pile face up in the middle. On "go" players turn over their card and look for a matching picture on the card in the middle. The first to spot and name a matching object takes the card from the pile in the middle and places it over his or her card face up. A new card is now revealed in the middle for players to find a matching item. The winner has the most cards at the end.

This is a fast game so there is no time for sentences. Use it for vocabulary revision. The rapid repetition of the vocabulary will significantly help students retain it as well as make them more motivated to pay attention in class in order to be better at the game.

What am I?

Category: Speaking – fluency activity
Group size: 2 to 30
Level: Intermediate to Advanced
Materials: Clothes pegs or sticky tape
Age: 8 to 12
Pace: Wake up

Cut out a product advertisement for each child in your group. Choose items children like such as Coke, Snickers, a teen magazine, KFC, Mac Donald's and M&Ms, or branch out into people and use sporting celebrities, cartoon characters or famous people. Alternatively ask pupils to secretly write someone or something down so you are sure to get products or people they know and relate to.

Give out a clothes peg to each child and have everyone stick their paper onto someone else's back without that person seeing the item. Give a few minutes time limit for everyone to figure out what is on their back by asking and answering questions. Children ask or answer anything other than directly asking "What am I?" Before the time limit starts, brainstorm with the class for suitable questions.

To keep the noise level contained tell children to whisper and any one talking loudly or speaking in the native language is out of the game.

What Time is it Mr. Wolf?

Category: Speaking - telling the time and/or meal times
Group size: Variants for all class sizes
Level: Beginner to Lower Intermediate
Materials: None
Age: 4 to 12 for meal times and 6 to 12 for telling the time
Pace: Various - see variants

Small group variant 1 - The classic game - suitable only for small groups in a 'summer camp' type environment.

The wolf walks slowly ahead with the children following behind. The pupils ask in unison "What's the time Mr. Wolf?" Mr. Wolf replies "It's one o'clock" (or whatever time he likes). The class repeat the question until Mr. Wolf replies, "It's dinner time!" At this point Mr. Wolf turns round and tries to catch one of the children. Swap Mr. Wolf over at this point, regardless of whether he has caught anyone.

Mr. Wolf can also call out breakfast time, lunchtime, teatime, suppertime, and even elevenses, (a British custom of coffee or tea with biscuits around 11am). Whenever Mr. Wolf calls out a time involving eating he turns and chases the group.

Classroom variant 2

One pupil is the wolf, who faces the board or away from the group. The class members stand behind their desks and ask in unison, "What time is it Mr. Wolf?" Mr. Wolf replies, "It's one o'clock". The class repeat the question until Mr. Wolf says, "It's dinner time!" At this point the children freeze and Mr. Wolf turns round to see if anyone is moving. Anyone caught moving becomes the new wolf.

See variant three for more time telling options. Combine this with variant three for more fun.

Classroom variant 3

One pupil is the wolf, facing away from the group. Pupils hold up 1 to 10 fingers, 1 arm in the air for 11 or two arms in the air for 12. The class asks in unison, "What time is it Mr. Wolf?" Mr. Wolf replies with a time, e.g. "It's 5 o'clock". Anyone holding up 5 fingers becomes the wolf. If more than one pupil has five then the wolf picks one of them out. Combine this with variant two for more fun and variety. To use more time telling possibilities use the following idea: 3 o'clock is three fingers held above the head. Quarter past 3 is three fingers held to the right of the body. Half past 3 is three fingers held over the stomach. Quarter to four is three fingers held to the left of the body.

Classroom variant 4 with flashcards

Pupils stand at their desks with a wolf up front. In this version, each class member has a flashcard with a different time on it. It's possible to ask pupils to draw a clock and choose a time themselves to have everyone kitted out with their own flashcard in minutes. If the wolf says, "It's half past five", anyone holding that time must call back, "It's half past five". The class keep their flashcards flat on their desks, or hidden from the wolf. The wolf then turns round and must identify who replied by the sound of their voice. If the wolf does this successfully that person becomes the next wolf. Or swap the wolf over every so often.

Classroom variant 5 with flashcards

This variant is a little more lively, but still very manageable. Students hold up their flashcards (see variant 4) to the wolf. The wolf mentally picks one of the times he sees and turns away from the class. The class asks in unison, "What time is it Mr. Wolf?" Mr.

Wolf says, "It's five o'clock", and then counts to four at a steady pace.

The class members holding "five o'clock" may, if they choose to, quickly swap their card, or give it to a neighbour before the wolf turns around. Every one freezes. On the count of 4 the wolf turns round and tries to catch someone moving. Anyone caught moving sits out the next round only, loses a point or does a forfeit. The wolf then names the person he believes to be holding the 5 o'clock card.

Where Is it?

Category: Listening
Group size: 2 to 40 in pairs or small groups
Level: Beginner to Advanced
Materials: Pen and paper or prepared pictures
Age: 5 to 12
Pace: Calm

The essence of this game is to describe something for the group to draw. For example tell students to draw a house with 4 rooms. Then describe what to draw in each room, such as "The bed is in the bedroom", or "In the bedroom is a double bed, with two pillows and a pink duvet cover", or "Draw a bed. There is a dog on the bed. There is a cat under the bed. Next to the bed there is a chair." Make it clear by a rapid demonstration sketch that this is not a Leonardo di Vinci competition and that speed is of the essence.

Children swap pictures and describe the picture to a partner. Children can also work in pairs with one child telling the other what to draw. If you have a mixed ability class put the children in groups and let the more advanced children describe a picture to their group.

This game suits prepositions and a broad range of vocabulary, as well as many different sentence structures. For intermediates tell a story in the past tense. Students draw the key elements of the story, enough so that they can re-tell it to a different group using their pictures as prompts.

Which One Has Gone?

Category: Speaking - naming vocabulary
Group size: 2 to 30
Level: Beginner to Advanced
Materials: One set of picture cards or objects per group
Age: 4 to 12
Pace: Wake up

Put up a set of picture cards on the board and ask pupils to close their eyes. To prevent cheating you could ask the children to fold their arms on their desks and put their head on their arms so they are all looking down at their desk. Take away one of the cards on the board and say, 'which one has gone?" When they hear this question the children look up, identify and name the missing picture as fast as possible. Take away more than one picture at a time if you wish. You can also move the pictures around in between goes - as long as you do this quickly so players are not kept waiting. Bring up the winners to remove pictures and ask the question to give the slower ones a chance to answer. With four year olds start with two pictures only and gradually add to them. As always with the very young have them everyone answer, with no emphasis on the pupil who answers first.

If possible divide your class into groups, giving each a set of pictures that children can lay out on the floor, or on tables. Each group needs a leader; so let the better students do this. All the players close their eyes, the leaders take away a card and ask in unison with you "Which one has gone?" In this way, although you are playing in groups, you control everyone's game. With teenage players and older let each group play at its own pace. Use any question for this game, not just "Which one has gone?" For example with food pictures use a question such as "What did I have for lunch today?"

Who Wants to be a Millionaire Adaptation

Category: Speaking

Group size: 2 to 20 students for best results. Can be played with 30 students too, but involves more waiting.
Level: Beginner to Intermediate
Materials: None
Age: 4 to Adult
Pace: Calm

Split the class into two teams. Draw two columns on the board with 5 squares in each. With smaller groups add more squares to the columns - up to 12 squares maximum. Stick a card below the lowest square or place a cross there with the board pen. Ask 5 students from the first team to stand up. Ask a question that includes the language you are working on. One of the students answers and if correct advance their cross or card up into the first box in the column. That student now sits down. Now ask the team if they want to continue or stop. If they elect to continue the teacher asks another question and one of the four students who are still standing answers it. If correct their cross or card advances one more square up the column and if incorrect the cross or card drops right back to the starting line. It is like in "Who Wants to Be a Millionaire" where one wrong answer means loss of all money won up to that point. Once that team have either elected to stop or given a wrong answer taking them back to the beginning it is the other team's turn.

With beginners ask easy questions such as: "What is your name?" With four and five year olds ask the same questions repeatedly, this is an excellent excuse to drill. The questions do not need to be general knowledge as you are testing English here.

This is excellent for small groups. With a large class watch out that the game does not drag and keep the questions coming rapidly. You could ask the team not answering questions to be busy writing questions out for the other team to answer during the next round. This keeps all students involved and actively participating rather than passively sitting waiting for a turn.

Word Challenge

Category: Spelling
Group size: Divide the class into teams of 4 to 6 students
Level: Beginner to Upper Intermediate
Materials: None
Age: 6 to Adult
Pace: Calm

Allow each team a few minutes to think up some words for the other team to spell. Students may consult their textbooks to come up with words on condition that these come from units already covered in class. Another rule is that students may only choose words that they know how to spell themselves. With more advanced classes it can be helpful to allow use of the dictionary.

Now put the teams together in groups of two teams. A student from team A says his or her word to team B. A student from team B must spell that word. If correct, team B win a point. Each student from team A takes a turn saying his or her word and a different student from team B takes a turn in spelling it. Students may ask their team members for help but no looking in the textbook is allowed.

An optional follow-up activity is for students to note any words spelled incorrectly and you make a list of those on the board, which the class copy down and learn for homework. In the next lesson play a round of *Word Challenge* with these words only and see how the teams do. The results will be better and the children will be more likely to remember the spellings longer term.

Word Flash Cards

Category: Reading and Speaking
Group size: 2 to 35
Level: Beginner
Materials: Picture flashcards
Age: 6 to 12
Pace: Calm

Divide the class into two teams and in the space of a minute hold up as many word flash cards as possible while the team names each one. Do the same for Team 2, with different words or the same ones in a different order, and see which team named the most.

The rule is that everyone on the team must name the word at the same time. Put this in place through a clapping rhythm: slap the top of the thighs with both hands at the same time, clap hands together in front of the chest, click the left thumb and middle finger, then click the right thumb and middle finger. If your pupils can't yet click their fingers give them another action instead. This will give you a four beat rhythm. During the thigh slap turn the word flash card over, and during the other three beats the team says the word.

You are the judge as to whether a word is well said or not. To pass you need the word said by at least half the team in a fairly convincing way. If you only have one or two pupils say the word, or it's somewhat muffled, then no point is awarded for that word! As you lay down the used words make two piles, one pile of points earned and the other that did not score so that it is easy to count up the team points.

Another idea is to have the children's names on cards in a bag on your desk. Every now and then you pull out a name, and that person must read the next word out, to get double points for their team. Only hold the word up for few seconds before hiding it again to keep interest and attention. If using word cards for spelling, for fun at the end of a game surprise the class by fishing out a giant word such as this one from Oliver Twist, "supercalifragilisticexpialidoscious".

Word Photographs

Category: Spelling
Group size: Any
Level: Beginner to Advanced
Materials: Board and pens
Age: 6 to 12
Pace: Flexible

The essence of this game is to look at word shapes as pictures as well as letters. Here is the technique: Look at the word and take a mental picture of it. Zoom in on the word, focus and then close your eyes and see the word in your head. Now ask yourself what the first letter of the word is, the last, and the third, and so on. With some training this technique will become automatic and the brain learns to photograph words, as well as hear the word as a sound. This helps exponentially with spelling.

To play reveal a word for five seconds (on the board or with a flashcard). Let children take their mental photograph. Then ask, "3rd letter?" and let the class call it out while a pupil comes to the board and writes up that letter. Continue through the entire word until it is written up in full. Swap the person over at the front doing the writing with each word, not each letter, so the game does not drag. Optionally use teams and have pupils race to the front to write up the letter you call out, as in *Team Race on the Board.*

Word Stress Chant and Spell

Category: Speaking and Spelling
Group size: any
Level: Beginner to Advanced
Materials: Board and pens
Age: 6 to 12 and variant without spelling for younger pupils
Pace: Calm

Read *Pronunciation Word Stress* first as background to this game. Here's another way to work on word stress. The teacher, or a pupil says the word with the correct stress. The class then chant this in unison correctly ten times and during that time three or four class members come up to the board, write out the word from memory and return to their seats before the chanting is up. Points go to teams where the word is spelled correctly and within the given time. This game gives lots of speaking time to the whole class at once while also working on spelling. Enhance the correct stress by having the whole class clap on the strong syllable each time.

With younger pupils or if you prefer not to do the spelling part then use the same idea but have pupils come up to the board and draw the item before the chanting is up.

Write It Up

Category: Writing
Group size: 2 to 35
Level: Beginner to Advanced
Materials: Board and pens
Age: 6 to 12
Pace: Wake up

Divide the class into teams and number the players in each team. Call out a word or a sentence followed by one of the team numbers, say number 3. All the number 3s walk or race to the board and write up the sentence. It doesn't matter if they copy from their classmates, this is not a cheat, but a learning experience. Have the class make sure the sentences written up are correct. While this is going on all pupils are thinking up a sentence to follow the one on the board, which would be a coherent follow-on. Call out another team number, say 1, the number 1s race up and write up their version of a follow-on sentence, and so on.

With complete beginners writing up sentences in this way may be too ambitious, so use single words instead. Pupils then write up any word that is related to the previous one.

Writing Race

Category: Writing
Group size: 2 to 40
Level: Beginner to Advanced
Materials: Pens and paper
Age: 6 to 12
Pace: Wake up

Here is an easy, fun writing game. Thanks to Debbie Pyle for this game idea. You need some room between desks in class to play. This game is to be played once your students are familiar with the target language and is particularly good for going over specific grammatical points or spelling. Use it to add a fun twist to worksheets.

Divide the class into pairs, threes or fours, but no more than four per group. Each group has two pencils, one worksheet and one blank piece of paper. On the word go the first child of each pair or group runs to the worksheet and fills in the blank/s for the first item on the worksheet. He or she then runs back to the blank piece of paper and writes the item out in full there. This may be the whole sentence or just the words that went into the blanks on the worksheet. The pencils stay with the worksheets so the children do not run with them.

As soon as soon as the first child reaches the blank piece of paper the second child can go to the worksheet and fill in the second item, leave the pencil on the desk and return to the blank piece of paper. The first child should have finished writing out the item by now, and either runs back to the worksheet to do the third item if working in pairs, or waits in line until his or her turn comes round again. Here is a concrete example of how that works. Using a worksheet for 'a/an' the first child runs to the worksheet and fills in item 1, in this case 'an' before elephant. The child then runs back to the blank piece of paper and writes out 'an elephant', while the second child runs to the worksheet and fills out item 2, 'a' before ball, and so on.

A variant is to have two worksheets instead of a blank piece of paper - either identical for reinforcing newly learned things, or different ones for revising a greater number of items. When the worksheets are all filled up the game is over. For marking children can mark their own in pairs or groups. Everyone has three lives so as you go through the answers students can rub out three incorrect answers and replace them with the correct ones. This means that it is highly likely the whole class will get 100%, which is great for the feel-good factor. In addition the fact of rubbing out the wrong answer and rewriting the correct one helps learning far better than a big red cross. If any children rub out more than 3 incorrect answers, let them and pretend you haven't noticed. If a child squeals on another you could say, "thank you for helping but in this case it would be better if you concentrated on your own worksheet". That has got to be better than putting the spotlight on the child who has got so many wrong answers that they have to keep rubbing them all out! Remember that the idea is for the children to learn, get high scores and enjoy English.

a or an?

Animals

1. _____ elephant
2. _____ tiger
3. _____ snake
4. _____ horse
5. _____ iguana
6. _____ animal

Body Parts

7. _____ mouth
8. _____ arm
9. _____ nose
10. _____ hand
11. _____ eye
12. _____ leg
13. _____ foot
14. _____ ear
15. _____ knee

Food

16. _____ banana
17. _____ potato
18. _____ apple
19. _____ carrot
20. _____ chocolate
21. _____ egg
22. _____ icecream
23. _____ sandwich
24. _____ cake

Other words

25. _____ house
26. _____ igloo
27. _____ tent
28. _____ umbrella
29. _____ bus
30. _____ orchestra

Language ideas to use with this game

This game lends itself to any language as long as it is short - being a writing race it isn't practical to have great long sentences to write out. However if you use 2 worksheets with fill in the blanks then the sentences can be as long as you like. If you wanted to reinforce spelling then have one worksheet which the children run to, memorise the first word, run back to the blank piece of paper and write that word down while the second child runs to the worksheet to memorise the second word, and so on. This idea could also be used for very short sentences or vocabulary.

Another spelling idea is to use a worksheet with pictures only. The child looks at the first picture, runs back to the blank piece of paper and writes down the word. Work on any language with fill in the blanks such as question forms, verb endings, parts of verbs, vocabulary, pronouns, etc.

Zambezi River

Category: Speaking
Group size: 2 to 12
Level: Beginner to Intermediate
Materials: Picture flashcards
Age: 4 to 10
Pace: Wake up

The Zambezi River flows over the Victoria Falls and below the rapids it is infested with crocodiles! The players have to get across the river without being eaten by the crocodiles. They do this by jumping from rock to rock or picture to picture and naming the pictures as they go. They have to name the picture, or say the sentence or question about the picture in order to carry onto the next rock and finally to safety.

Language can be simple vocabulary to sentences or questions. For example all the players ask in unison "Where are you going?" and the player crossing the Zambezi says, "I'm going to the beach, I'm going to the circus, I'm going to the zoo", as he or she steps on pictures of the beach, the circus and the zoo.

Younger children can be quite perturbed by the prospect of being eaten by the crocodile, which is real in their imagination, and therefore I never eat four year olds, or allow them to be eaten by the other crocodiles (who are the other players). I have even seen 9 years old children on the verge of tears at the prospect of being eaten, but I have seen other 6 years olds deliberately get the word wrong just so that they can be eaten. Be sensitive to each individual - you don't want him or her in tears.

Groups may be split into two teams with one team as the crocodiles while the other team help their members across. How you go about eating your players depends on whether you are in a formal classroom situation, or whether you are more relaxed with your students - I leave it to your imagination!

Zip Zap Vocabulary Revision

Category: Speaking
Group size: 6 to 30
Level: Beginner to Intermediate
Materials: Picture flash cards
Age: 5 to 12
Pace: Wake up

Game One

Ideally seat children in a circle. Each child has a different picture flashcard that is clearly displayed for all players to see. Start by calling out one of the words - for example bananas. The child with the picture of bananas must immediately name another picture in the circle, such as apples. The child with the apples in turn names another picture, any one, except for bananas, and so on.

With more than 15 children call out two pictures, such as bananas and apples, so that two children then name two new words. This increases the speaking opportunities and ensures that all the children listen attentively, whereas with only one word to thirty children the pace would be too slow and the game boring.

If you notice that the same words are being called out over and over again then when a word has been named the child holding that card must turn it face down so it cannot be called again in that round. Either give that child another card or wait until all the cards are face down, then have the children swap their cards over and play again.

If you have to play with children at their desks then play as above except that children hold their picture cards up to the person who has a turn at naming a card. If you have two or three words being batted about simultaneously then the children have to do their best to show their card to those children. As long as those who must name a word can see some pictures to choose from the game will work.

Game Two – Better for 6 to 20 pupils

Players each hold a picture card and form a circle. One player stands in the middle of the circle. In turn everyone then names his or her picture while each person tries to remember the cards on his immediate left and right. The player in the middle then points a finger at one of the players in the circle and says ZIP-1,2,3,4,5. The child being pointed at must then name the card on his or her left without looking at it. If successful the person in the middle repeats the exercise with another child. If unsuccessful that child swaps places with the player in the middle. If the player in the middle says ZAP-1,2,3,4,5 then the child being pointed at must name the picture card on his or her right. An easier variant for those who do not yet know left and right is to name any one word on ZIP-1,2,3,4,5 and any two words on ZAP-1,2,3,4,5.

TECHNOLOGY AND MULTI MEDIA

Thoughts on Technology and Multi-Media

This section contains ideas about using the Internet and technology in class and for homework. I learned some of these ideas at a big TEFL conference where I was also speaking. The lecture was on technology and the 21st century ESL classroom and the speaker was from IATEFL Hungary.

To carry out these ideas you need to be very well equipped with computers at school and possibly at home, and children need digital cameras. However take heart, because if your school is not kitted out like the Star Trek Enterprise you can stay abreast of developments nonetheless!

The buzz in teaching today is all about the "21st century" classroom, integrating technology and producing students who are ready to go into the work place. In order to close the gap between what employers are looking for and what is being taught in school teachers, in addition to English, should teach: Professionalism, work ethic, critical thinking, team work, technology, leadership, creativity, cross-cultural understanding and self-direction.

You are probably thinking; "oh boy and I was having trouble with the present tense." But even if you feel daunted including technology in class or for homework tasks, it can enhance your teaching no end. Variety is the spice of life and including technology adds to the mix. Many students will be far more motivated to prepare a personal biography using photos from home on PowerPoint than they will filling in a gap fill or a worksheet on some random family members in a textbook. So here are some of the ways to integrate technology into your classroom, which also allow for the development of other attributes on the above list. If students are learning computer skills as part of their curriculum liaise with the IT teacher and see how you could work together on one of the projects below.

Making a Class Blog

Set up a social network for the classroom. Only the administrator can invite new members which ensures that only your class is on the network. The administrator controls content to ensure the site stays clean and on purpose. There is a forum section where class members post topics and comments - all in English of course. Post homework up there so if someone misses class they can log on from home. Post class projects, stories, upload photos, videos, put birthdays up there and create a class blog.

It's straight forward to sign up and someone in your class might love to help you set up the blog. Type “make a blog for the classroom” into your preferred search engine and many helpful sites will come up. Alternatively create a dedicated Facebook page for the class.

Quiz Websites

Use a quiz site to make quizzes and play online word games and multiple choice. There are excellent vocabulary games on there and the children may work at their own pace. One such site is www.quizlet.com - a search on the net will yield others.

Making Picture Clips with Music

Children make short picture clips with music by uploading three pictures and choosing the music. These sequences can be about anything, such as my favourite movie, family life, my ideal holiday, my best friend, my favourite band, or whatever topic engages your pupils. If you don't know then ask them! These clips can be uploaded onto the class blog or social network and shared. Set homework asking the children to decide which movie gets the Oscar and why and so on. Let the children make up bizarre stories based on the clips. The kids may comment on the videos in the forum.

Since things change fast on the web, rather than referring to sites today that will be out of date tomorrow, type "free slideshow video maker with music" into Google and you'll find the latest offerings.

Making Movies

Children need a camera or a phone with a camera at home to do this assignment. Children work in groups so that they learn cooperation and get around any issues with some children not having home access to a camera. The example shown at a conference by IATEFL Hungary was a truly funny and inspiring video that had been made by a group of four children aged ten as a project to explain hand symbols. They had picked hand symbols used for scuba divers. One filmed, one narrated and two acted out the symbols, fully equipped with diving masks, snorkels and standing behind an aquarium one of them had in their home! That film clearly let the children use their creativity, work together as a team, learn something new and work independently of the teacher. What an ideal way to engage your class.

If you have the time and facilities, software packages such as Windows Media or iMovie allow the uploading of films which can then be put to music, and subtitled. Fancy effects can easily be created to switch between scenes. If you have limited time with the class then do consider whether one is teaching English or IT as the uploading of films and so on is extremely time-consuming. It may be more appropriate as a homework task.

Slide Shows

PowerPoint is an easy-to-use software where pupils upload pictures, music and add subtitles to slides. Pupils could prepare and present it in English. Easy topics where students will have pictures available are my family, an interview with a friend or family member, my friends, my school, my pet, my hobby, my home, my last holiday, my favourite movie and my favourite music band.

Help students by providing a framework or outline for them to fill in with their own specific topic. For example, introduce the main characters, describe where the topic or story takes place and write down the main events/questions. Next assemble relevant pictures and music. Finally students rehearse their narration as they show their pictures and play their choice of music. Allow time for pupils to run through these in class and consider showing them to other classes and to parents as part of an after-school show or event.

What if you are teaching in a yak tent?

Take heart if you have no electricity in your school. All these activities described are about human beings communicating with each other, and we've been doing that for a long time. My personal view is that the use of computers, websites and digital cameras is just the packaging for the activity which your pupils will find cool and relevant. You can use all these ideas just as well by adapting them.

Many teachers are in remote areas and do not have access to cameras, the internet and so on, making it impossible to implement the above ideas. But they can all be adapted. Never fear, we can be creative without internet and without techie gadgets!

Make a big notice board instead of the blog. Kids stick up their comments and pictures on pieces of paper. Use the picture clips with music idea using three pictures that children draw or cut out from old magazines. Tell children to prepare short plays to perform in front of the class instead of filming them and showing the class on a screen. For those of you in countries where you do have access to the web then go ahead and give these ideas a go. For those of you in tepees, take the spirit of these ideas and apply them creatively.

Once the novelty value of using gadgets and software wears off many students will learn better with real photos, paper and glue and by writing out labels by hand because they are primarily tactile or kinaesthetic learners.

The true value in these ideas is that they lead pupils to be creative, to work in a team, to be responsible for their own learning, to work independently from the teacher, to express themselves and to feel part of the learning process by actively participating in it.

RHYMES RIDDLES AND PROVERBS

Rhymes help with confidence and fluency, and allow syntax and grammar to be absorbed subconsciously. Children also love them, and they provide an opportunity to use vocabulary words learned in the context of sentences, which is satisfying. Use rhymes with sophisticated tenses and language right from beginner three year olds. First teach some of the vocabulary found in the rhyme with games, and then introduce the rhyme. With repetition, and exposure to the rhyme over a series of lessons, perhaps using the same rhyme in a different game or setting, you will find that the children will learn it over time. Use miming with rhymes and songs whenever you can, especially with the young ones. Make up actions yourself and ask the class for ideas for actions - you'll get some good ideas that way!

It dip doo
The dog's got the flu,
The cat's got chicken pox
and out go you!

Three blind mice,
Three blind mice,
See how they run,
See how they run,
They all ran off to the farmer's wife
Who cut off their tails with a carving knife

The three blind mice.

I like coffee,
I like tea.
I like the boys
and the boys like me.
Yes,
No,
Maybe so.
Yes,
No,
Maybe so.

One banana, two bananas, three bananas, four,
Five bananas, six bananas, seven bananas, more.

Mirror mirror on the wall, who is the fairest of them all? (From Snow White)

This is a finger play starting with the thumb and working around to the little finger. When the piggy goes "wee wee wee all the way home" you may tickle the child if he or she likes it.

This little piggy went to market,
This little piggy stayed at home,
This little piggy had roast beef,
This little piggy had none,
And this little piggy went wee wee wee wee wee
All the way home!
Hickory dickory dock,
The mouse ran up the clock.
The clock struck one
The mouse ran down,
Hickory dickory dock

One two
Buckle my shoe,

Three four
Knock on the door,
Five Six
Pick up sticks,
Seven eight
Lay them straight,
Nine ten
Big fat hen.

Eeny meeny miney mo,
Catch a piglet by its toe.
If it squeals let it go,
Eeny meeny miney mo,
O. U. T. spells out so out you must go!

Porridge in a pot, porridge in a pot,
Hubble bubble, hubble bubble, hot, hot, hot!

Milk in a mug, milk in a mug,
Drink it up, drink it up, glug, glug, glug!

Ickle ockle blue bockle,
Fishes in the sea,
If you want a pretty maid,
Please choose me.

Humpty Dumpty sat on a wall,
Humpty Dumpty had a great fall,
All the king's horses and all the king's men,
Couldn't put Humpty together again.

Handy Pandy Jack a Dandy
Loved plum cake and sugar candy.
He went into the baker's shop,
Then out he came, hop, hop, hop.

Hey diddle diddle, the cat and the fiddle,

The cow jumped over the moon.
The little dog laughed to see such fun,
And the dish ran away with the spoon.

Here comes a caterpillar, here comes a snail,
Here comes a slug with a slippery trail.
Here comes a butterfly, here comes a bee,
How many insects can you see?

One for a seesaw, two for a slide,
Three for the bike I like to ride.
Four for a go-kart, five for a swing,
Six for a kite on a long, long string.

Sally goes round the sun,
Sally goes round the moon,
Sally goes round the chimney pots
On a Saturday afternoon

Riddles for children

Bearing in mind that most of these involve a play on words and good vocabulary they are best for intermediate levels. Use these with adults too.

Why did the chicken cross the road? Because it wanted to get to the other side.
Can giraffes have babies? No, they can only have giraffes.
What does a house wear? Address.
What did the sock say to the foot? You're putting me on.
How do rabbits travel? By Hare plane.
What shoes should you wear when your basement is flooded? Pumps.
What kind of ties can't you wear? Railroad ties.
Why are potatoes good detectives? Because they always keep their eyes peeled.
Why was the belt arrested? For holding up the trousers (or pants

US).
What kind of eyeglasses do spies wear? Spy-focals.
What do you get when you saw a comedian in two? A half-wit.
When is it dangerous to play cards? When the joker is wild.
What does the invisible man drink at snack time? Evaporated milk.
What kind of soda must you not drink? Baking soda.
What part of your body has the most rhythm? Your eardrums.
How does mother earth fish? With North and South poles.
Where is the ocean the deepest? On the bottom.
Where is the best place to see a man-eating fish? In a seafood restaurant.
What do whales like to chew? Blubber gum.
What did the beach say when the tide came in? Long time no sea.
What did one potato chip say to the other? Shall we go for a dip?
What did the chocolate bar say to the lollipop? Hello sucker.
How does a king open a door? With a monarchy.
What do you need to spot an iceberg 20 miles away? Good eyesight!
What did the dog say to the little child pulling his tail? That is the end of me.
What horse never goes out in the daytime? A nightmare.
Where do animals go when they lose their tails? To a retail store.
What is the best year for a kangaroo? A leap year

Proverbs

A bird in the hand is worth two in the bush
A friend in need is a friend indeed
A miss is as good as a mile
A penny saved is a penny earned
A rolling stone gathers no moss
A stitch in time saves nine
A watched pot never boils
A word to the wise is sufficient
Absence makes the heart grow fonder
Actions speak louder than words
All roads lead to Rome

All that glitters is not gold
An apple a day keeps the doctor away
April showers bring May flowers
Beggars can't be choosers
Birds of a feather flock together
Blood is thicker than water
Don't count your chickens until they're hatched
There's no use crying over spilt milk
Every cloud has a silver lining
Familiarity breeds contempt
Half a loaf is better than none
Handsome is as handsome does
Heaven helps those who help themselves
Honesty is the best policy
Horses for courses
Let sleeping dogs lie
Look before you leap
Make hay while the sun shines
Necessity is the mother of invention
One man's meat is another's man's poison
Out of the frying pan, into the fire
Practice makes perfect
Rome wasn't built in a day
Strike while the iron is hot
The early bird catches the worm
The pen is mightier than the sword
There's no place like home

LESSON PLANS

Contact Shelley Ann Vernon for the lesson plans included with this book: info@teachingenglishgames.com

Details of lesson plans included free with this book:

1. Alphabet 1
2. Alphabet 2
3. Body parts 1
4. Body parts 2
5. Clothing + what are you wearing?
6. Clothing + what colour is?
7. Clothing + what is he/she wearing?
8. Directions
9. Food + I like / I don't like
10. Food + Do you like? Yes I do.
11. Food + Would you like?
12. Food – Revision
    Food – The Best Restaurant Play Script
13. Numbers 1-10 and colours
14. Numbers 1-20, How many? What colour is?
15. Professions + what do you do?
16. Professions + what does he/she do?

Also included: 20 worksheets for the above themes

OTHER RESOURCES

I hope that this book of games brings much joy to your classrooms as it has for thousands of other teachers. Here are my other resources, which may be useful if you teach a variety of ages or class sizes.

1. Preschool Games and Stories 1 to 10 for ages 3 to 6

Ten stories covering basic vocabulary themes and useful vocabulary with a fun games book for preschoolers. In paperback on Amazon and in PDF instant download from TeachingEnglishGames.com

www.teachingenglishgames.com/esl-short-stories

Email Shelley Ann Vernon for a free sample story on info@teachingenglishgames.com

2. English for Toddlers Report:

How to Teach English as a Second Language to two year old children. PDF downloadable report from: info@teachingenglishgames.com

3. Teaching English Songs 1 2 and 3 - CDs or Download

CD with sixteen songs to match the vocabulary taught in my preschool stories series. The words are simple, covering basic vocabulary themes, helping you to reinforce what you are teaching while bringing cheerful music to the classroom.

A songs activity book is included with CD 1, lesson plan ideas for introducing and teaching each song. These ideas may be used with any songs in the series. In addition masks of all the characters in the story are included in black and white, to cut out, colour and wear, and pre-coloured.

www.teachingenglishgames.com/eslsongs.htm

4. Follow-on Stories 11 to 20 with Lesson Plans

More stories covering actions, family members, rooms of the house, nature, light and dark, verbs, farm animals, body parts, clothing and other useful vocabulary.

In paperback on Amazon and in PDF instant download from TeachingEnglishGames.com

www.teachingenglishgames.com/kindergarten-stories

5. Stories for Special Days in the Year

Stories with lesson plans, flashcards, colouring and illustrations. In paperback on Amazon or instant download.

Birthday	Ground hog Day	April Fools' Day
Halloween	Valentine's Day	Mother's Day
Thanksgiving	Easter Bunny	Christmas
Summer Holiday Adventure		

Includes revision of vocabulary and grammar from stories one to twenty, plus new words, language and tenses.

www.teachingenglishgames.com/eslstory.htm

6. Teen/Adult Games book

This includes games and activities for all levels. Printable board games and game cards are provided to keep preparation to a minimum. In paperback and Kindle on Amazon and in PDF from TeachingEnglishGames.com

www.teachingenglishgames.com/esl-for-adults

7. One to One Games and Video Demonstration

Games for private tutors and parents with video demonstrations for ages 6 to 12.

www.teachingenglishgames.com/how-to-teach-a-child-to-speak-english

In paperback on Amazon and in PDF from TeachingEnglishGames.com

8. Plays and Skits for Children

30 simple repetitive skits with a touch of humour.

Plays and skits for small groups up to 15 students. With good classroom management the skits may be used with two groups of children working separately.

For beginners learning English and easily adapted to higher levels.

Private tutors or parents may also use these for one on one.

In paperback and Kindle on Amazon and in PDF from

www.teachingenglishgames.com/eslplays.htm

9. Primary School Curriculum of Stories

Level: Prepares for CEF A1, ILR 0/0+, ACTFL NL. Texts in UK and US versions with two levels of text.
Age Range: 6 to 10.
Email the author for a free sample:
info@teachingenglishgames.com

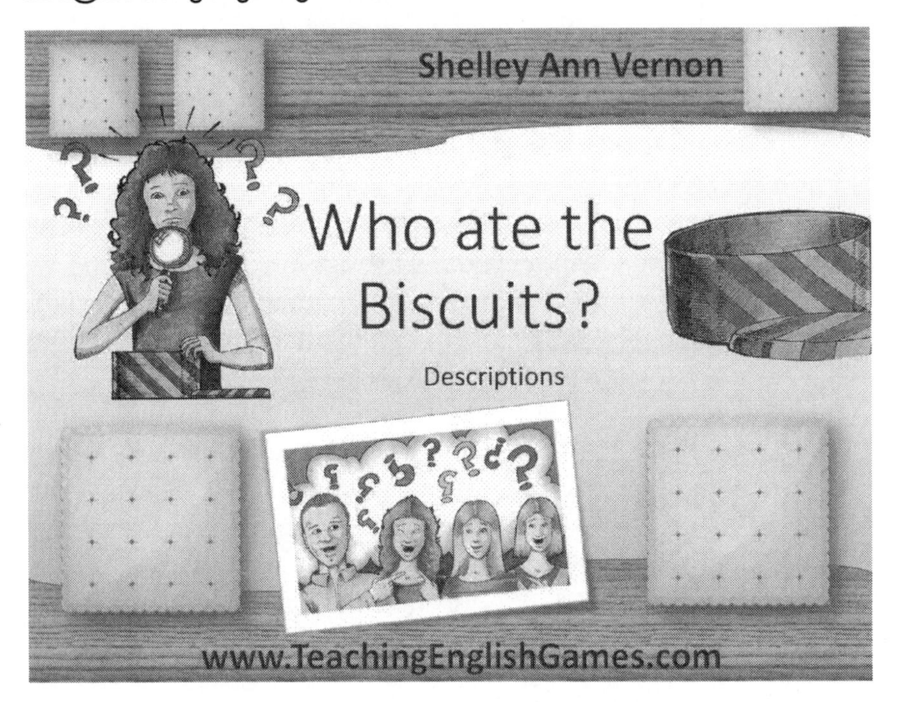

ABOUT THE AUTHOR

Following her BA degree in languages at Durham University, England in 1989 Shelley Vernon took a TEFL qualification and became a teacher. She taught in language schools in the UK and privately around the world for several years.

Having been largely bored to death herself while in school Shelley was determined not to put her own students through the same desperate clock-watching and she always strove to prepare fun, stimulating lessons that pupils would enjoy and remember. She taught using a variety of methods, including the driest textbooks imaginable, which called for creativity in order to make lessons more interesting. However it was only when she started to teach children French as a second language in 1999 that she really discovered the joy of teaching.

She created a method from her experiences and has shared her ideas with tens of thousands of teachers around the world, bringing enthusiasm and a love of learning into the classroom, as well as achieving great results. Shelley's approach concentrates on enhancing listening and speaking skills through language games which involve repetition and through fluency activities which have genuine communicative value rather than artificial conversation.

She created her best-selling "176 English Language Games for Children" and followed this with resources for preschool children, including games and a curriculum laid out in twenty illustrated stories. Having taught preschool children at a Montessori nursery school Shelley knows exactly what a teacher needs to be successful and stories are also a success with teachers worldwide. Her ESL Games and Activities for Adults have helped thousands of teachers worldwide.

In addition to her degree in foreign languages, Shelley holds a university degree in music (2000) from Canterbury Christchurch College. She loves classical music, and enjoys keeping fit with skiing, yoga and walking her adorable cocker spaniel. She also writes songs and has 3 preschool songs CDs. She speaks occasionally at conferences such as IATEFL Cardiff 2009, YALS

Belgrade 2011, UCN, Hjorring, Denmark and Barcelona 'Exams Catalunya' in November 2015.

INDEX OF GAMES

Made in the USA
San Bernardino, CA
15 September 2015